GOLF
SKILLS

GOLF
SKILLS

KEY TIPS AND TECHNIQUES TO IMPROVE YOUR GAME

LONDON, NEW YORK, MUNICH,
MELBOURNE, DELHI

Senior Editor	Bob Bridle
Senior Art Editor	Sharon Spencer
Production Editor	Tony Phipps
Production Controller	Louise Minihane
Jacket Designer	Nigel Wright
Managing Editor	Stephanie Farrow
Managing Art Editor	Lee Griffiths

DK INDIA

Managing Art Editor	Ashita Murgai
Editorial Lead	Saloni Talwar
Senior Art Editor	Rajnish Kashyap
Project Designer	Ivy Roy
Project Editor	Neha Gupta
Designers	Avani Parikh, Neetika Vilash
Editors	Pallavi Singh, Bincy Mathew
Production Manager	Pankaj Sharma
DTP Manager	Balwant Singh
Senior DTP Designer	Harish Aggarwal
DTP Designers	Shanker Prasad, Anita Yadav, Nand Kishor Acharya
Managing Director	Aparna Sharma

First published in Great Britain in 2011 by
Dorling Kindersley Limited
80 Strand, London WC2R 0RL

Penguin Group (UK)
2 4 6 8 10 9 7 5 3 1
001 – 176102 – March 2011

Includes content previously published in
The Complete Golf Manual

A CIP catalogue record for this book
is available from the British Library

ISBN 978-1-4053-4989-5

Printed and bound by
L. Rex Printing Company Limited, China

Discover more at www.dk.com

Contents

Introduction

The fact that this book is now in your hands suggests that you are aware of golf's addictive nature. While it may be clichéd to boast of golf's varied playing arena or the merits of the handicapping system, these are undeniably two of the attributes that make golf special.

But it is the physical act of playing, along with the mind games, that is so compelling. Even on a bad day, there may be a glimpse of magic – the experience of hitting a great shot or holing a long putt – that lifts your spirits and keeps you coming back for more. It is this "high" that fuels the desire to become a better player.

The early days

Ever since the first ball was struck (as early as the 16th century), people have striven to find a way of getting from a teeing ground to a hole with as few strokes as possible.

In golf's early days, swing technique was shaped mainly out of circumstance rather than choice. The earliest proper courses (which probably date from the 17th century) were almost certainly the coastal links in Scotland. There, it was discovered that a rounded swing, in which the hands and arms swing the club on a flat plane around the body, produced a low ball-flight and plenty of run. This suited the windswept landscape of the Scottish coast.

As photographs of the great players of the late 19th century confirm, playing in a tweed jacket and tie (as was the tradition in the early years) would have restricted arm movement, hampering a free, up-and-down swing of the hands and arms. Also, even up until the late 19th century, the likes of Mungo Park, Old Tom Morris, and Allen Robertson would stand with their feet nearly twice as far apart as today's top golfers, with their knees bent more than is usual nowadays, and with the ball way back in the stance (even for the driving clubs).

STUNNING SURROUNDINGS
Golf is a game played amid breathtaking scenery. The Cypress Point course on Monterey Peninsula, California, is a classic example.

Home-crafted equipment

Many of the top players of the 19th and early 20th century crafted with their own hands the tools that they wielded to such great effect. But, by today's standards, these clubs and balls appear primitive. Clubs were wooden-shafted, and the leather-wrapped handles called for a grip unlike the overlapping and interlocking methods employed today. Up until the mid-19th century, golf balls were made of stitched leather stuffed with feathers. They were expensive and would deform once wet. By the latter part of the century, balls were being made of gutta-percha, a rubber-like substance secreted from percha trees. "Gutties" flew better, but they could not be spun like today's high-tech balls.

The modern game

By the early part of the 20th century, the swing became more athletic and elegant. Bobby Jones advocated a narrow stance and golfers soon started to stand more upright, with their feet closer together. Byron Nelson's upright swing was best suited to the new steel-shafted clubs. In the 1980s, coach David Leadbetter popularized a swing less upright than the one used by Jack Nicklaus. It synchronized body and arm movement and today, most golfers finish their swing in a rounded position.

The role of the coach

Today's great teachers – such as David Leadbetter, Butch Harmon, and John Jacobs – work on essentially the same principles, but each applies individuality and different communication methods to the coaching role. While the standard of golf teaching has improved and become more uniform, golfers of all standards have grown increasingly receptive to tuition.

Your personal coach

Today, there is not a single golfer who does not want to shoot lower scores. Alas, most do not have a personal swing guru to turn to in times of need. This book intends to fulfil that role. Modern instruction is based on wisdom passed down from teachers over the years – from Harry Vardon to Butch Harmon. The exercises here expand upon this wealth of golfing knowledge. They are designed to cure faults and promote the right moves, ensuring that your sessions have clearly defined goals. Each aspect of the game is covered here – from tee shots to putting; from shotmaking to etiquette. The overall flow of the book is logical, and every page works hard so that you gain maximum benefit from the advice given. Specially commissioned photographs focus on details of the movements required for a perfect technique. The greatest satisfaction in golf comes from self-improvement, and this book will show you how to fully realize your golfing potential.

The Basics

The rules

Golf has more rules than most other sports, as there is more scope for incident on a 40-ha (100-acre) plot of varied landscape than there is, for example, on a tennis court. A basic understanding of the rules is given here, so that you can enjoy the game better.

On the tee

EXCESS BAGGAGE
Before you begin, check the number of clubs in your bag. If it exceeds 14, you will be penalized. In a matchplay competition, you will have to deduct one hole for every hole played with an extra club, up to a maximum of two holes. In a strokeplay event, you are penalized two strokes for each hole played with the extra clubs.

PLAYING OUT OF TURN
In a strokeplay event, if you play out of turn, there is no penalty, but it is poor etiquette. However, if you do so in a matchplay event, your opponent can ask you to play the stroke again.

OUTER LIMITS
Two tee markers indicate the width of the teeing area. You can't move these, but you can stand either side of them, providing the ball is teed up within the area. If you play from outside the area, the penalty varies depending on the type of game.

ACCIDENTAL NUDGE
If, when you address the ball, you accidentally nudge it off the tee-peg with the clubhead, there is no penalty. You simply place the ball back on the tee-peg and start again.

TROUBLE OFF THE TEE
If you lose your ball off the tee, or hit your tee shot out-of-bounds, use the illustrations on the right to help you work out the correct procedure to follow and the appropriate penalty to add to your score.

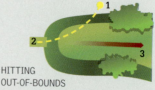

HITTING OUT-OF-BOUNDS

1 Your tee shot is wildly off line, and the ball disappears out-of-bounds.

2 You have now incurred a stroke-and-distance penalty. You must play another shot from the tee.

3 As long as this tee shot stays "in bounds", it counts as your third.

PLAYING A PROVISIONAL BALL

1 Your first shot lands in deep rough, and you fear that it might be lost.

2 Play a provisional ball if you can't find the first within five minutes. Add two penalty strokes to your score.

3 Because of the penalty strokes, the next shot is your fourth.

Striking the ball

A stroke is defined as the forward momentum of the club made with the intention of fairly striking at and moving the ball. It is useful to recall this description when considering what to do, for example, if you play an air shot. A legal strike of the ball also requires a backswing: you cannot scoop or push a ball towards the target.

Hazards

BUNKERS

The number one rule in sand is to hover the clubhead above the surface, as touching the sand before playing a shot incurs a one-shot penalty. There are, however, finer points to consider with bunker play. If the clubhead touches the sand in your backswing, you are penalized as you would be at address.

PENALTY DROP

When you face an unplayable lie (where you can't play a shot because of ground conditions or an obstruction, such as balls hit under pine trees, or into rocky areas), opt for a penalty drop. First, signal your intentions to one of your playing partners or the opponent. As you make the drop, stand upright with your arm extended in front of you at shoulder height, and let the ball fall out of your hand and drop to the ground. Do not influence its flight. If it comes to rest nearer the hole, re-drop. If this happens again, place the ball on any lie, choosing a position within two club-lengths of the original spot.

FREE DROP

You can make a free drop ("free relief"), in cases where, for example, the ground is damaged or there are immovable obstructions. But although a free drop does not incur a penalty, you are allowed a relief of only one club-length.

PLAYING THE WRONG BALL

It is against the rules to play a stroke with a ball that is not your own. In matchplay, the penalty is the loss of the hole, while in strokeplay, you receive a two-shot penalty and must take your next shot from where you played the wrong ball. If you fail to do so, you are disqualified from the competition.

WATER HAZARDS

There are two types of water hazard on a golf course: "water hazards" (marked with a yellow stake or a yellow painted line) and "lateral water hazards" (indicated by red stakes or a red painted line).

Whenever your ball finishes in water, identify which of the two hazards you are dealing with, as the procedures for each vary slightly.

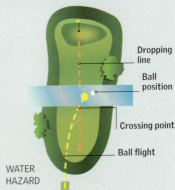

Dropping line

Ball position

Crossing point

Ball flight

WATER HAZARD

1 You may play the ball in the water – without incurring a penalty. But as you address the ball, the club must not touch the water.

2 A safer option is to drop the ball on an imaginary line running from the target through the point at which your ball first crossed the edge of the hazard. However, this incurs a one-stroke penalty.

Dropping line

Drop zone 1

Ball flight

Drop zone 2

Crossing point

LATERAL WATER HAZARD

1 You may take a drop of two club-lengths from where the ball first crossed the water-edge. Do not give yourself a lie closer to the hole.

2 If the first option is not practical, you may drop a ball as described in the step above, except on the other side of the hazard.

On the green

WHAT YOU CAN DO ON THE GREEN

If you want to clean your ball before putting, mark it by placing a coin or ball-marker behind the ball before lifting it away. You can replace a damaged ball with a new one, providing your opponent agrees. If your ball-marker interferes with the line of an opponent's putt, use your putterhead to measure as far to the side as is necessary and re-mark (see right). Put the marker back before you replace the ball.

WHAT YOU CAN'T DO ON THE GREEN

To avoid breaking rules on the green, remember to not touch the putt-line, unless you are brushing aside loose impediments, repairing a pitch-mark, or measuring distance to determine whose putt should be played first. Do not test the putting surface by rolling a ball along the green. Avoid hitting your putt while another ball is in motion. And, don't brush aside dew from the putt-line.

FLAGSTICK MISDEMEANOURS

If you are far from the hole, you will probably choose to have the flagstick attended (so you can see where the hole is). The flag must be pulled out before your ball goes in the hole. If you remove the flagstick, keep it out of the way, as there is a two-stroke penalty if it is hit.

MOVING THE MARKER

You should move your marker if it is on the line of another player's putt or if it interferes with the stroke or stance of another player. The procedure outlined below will show you the correct way to do this.

POSITION THE CLUB
To move your ball-marker away, place the toe of your putterhead so that it sits next to the marker.

MOVE THE MARKER
Position the marker behind the heel of the putterhead. Move several putterhead-lengths away if needed.

Unusual ground conditions

CASUAL WATER

Always play the ball as it lies, but there are exceptions to this rule. One such scenario is if your ball lands in casual water – a temporary accumulation of water. This is a free-drop scenario, and whenever possible, identify the original ball-position, mark the nearest point of relief with a tee, and drop within one club-length of the tee in any direction. If the water is in a bunker, identify a dry patch (within the confines of the bunker) on which to drop the ball. If the bunker is waterlogged, either drop the ball into the shallowest area or drop it outside the bunker and incur a one-stroke penalty.

GROUND UNDER REPAIR

A portion of the course that would be damaged if played on, can be declared "ground under repair" and encircled by a white line. If the ball lands inside this line, measure one club-length from the point where it is no longer an interference, and take your drop.

PLUGGED BALL

When a ball plugs in its own pitch-mark on a mown area of grass, you're allowed a free drop. Mark the ball-position, clean it, and drop it as close as possible to where it became plugged. You are not permitted a free drop in the rough.

Obstacles

LOOSE IMPEDIMENTS
Movable natural objects such as leaves and stones are loose impediments. If the object is not growing and is not solidly embedded in the ground, you can move it without penalty. But you will be penalized one shot if the ball moves as you clear the object away (unless you are on the green). You can't move loose impediments in a hazard. An exception to this rule is that you can move stones from around the ball in a bunker. Sand and loose soil are impediments if found on the green, but not off it.

IMMOVABLE OBSTRUCTIONS
Obstructions are artificial objects and include fixed sprinkler heads around greens and concrete tee boxes to the side of a teeing area. If these interfere with your stance or intended swing, you are entitled to free relief. You are not allowed relief if the obstruction is in the flightpath of your next shot.

MOVABLE OBSTRUCTIONS
Empty cans and bunker rakes are movable obstructions. If your ball comes to rest touching any of these or in such close proximity that it interferes with your stance or swing, you may move the obstruction. Mark the ball-position with a tee.

Deflected balls

BALL IN MOTION
If your ball is deflected while it is in motion, the correct procedure varies according to the cause of the deflection. If your ball hits something natural, such as a tree, play the ball from where it comes to rest. The same is true if your ball hits an "outside agency", such as a mower. If an animal intercepts your ball while it is in motion, replace it on the spot from where it was first taken. If your moving ball hits one at rest, you must play your ball from wherever it finishes. If it happens on the green, you incur a penalty.

STATIONARY BALL DEFLECTED
If your ball, while at rest, is moved by an outside agency, such as an animal, replace the ball as close as possible to the spot from where it was moved (there is no penalty). Even if the ball disappears, place a new ball where the original had been, and proceed without penalty. The rules are not so benevolent if a ball is moved by you, your caddie, partner, or any piece of equipment belonging to you or your partner. In this situation there is a one-stroke penalty, and you must replace the ball in its original position.

MOVING A BALL WHILE SEARCHING FOR IT INCURS A PENALTY

Choosing the right equipment

Enormous advances in technology over recent years have left consumers spoilt for choice when it comes to club selection. The market has never been more exciting or more confusing. The sheer variety of clubs available, the accompanying jargon, and the advanced construction materials used can sometimes make it difficult to make the right equipment-buying decisions.

Drivers

When purchasing a driver, consider the elements that influence a club's playability. First, the size of the clubhead; big clubheads provide a larger hitting area than small ones. The loft on the club is also critical. Powerful ball-strikers can manage with a loft of only seven degrees. But the height of your shots also depends on the club's centre of gravity. Clubs with a low centre of gravity help the ball become airborne, which suit the less-accomplished player. Other clubs have a higher centre of gravity, which give a more penetrating ball-flight.

FACE FACTS

Most drivers are made of steel. But titanium, although more expensive, is also popular, as it is light. The clubhead can be bigger and thus more forgiving.

MAKE SURE THAT THE GRIP FITS YOUR HANDS

A club's grip tends to be overlooked by many golfers, yet it is the only point of contact between you and the club. Therefore, it makes sense that the grip should suit your hands. Apart from keeping grips in good condition – replacing them when they become shiny or smooth – you also need to make sure that they are the correct size. Perform this simple test. Hold a club in your left hand. Ideally your middle two fingers should lightly touch the fleshy pad at the base of your thumb. If they do not touch at all, or the tips of your fingers dig into your palm, your grips need adjusting. This is a straightforward job that can be done by any club professional.

CORRECT GRIP SIZE

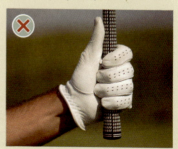

INCORRECT GRIP SIZE

FINDING THE CORRECT LIE ANGLE

The angle at which the bottom edge of the club sits on the ground is the lie angle. If this is too upright, the heel will make contact with the ground first at impact. Conversely, if the angle is too flat, the toe of the club will strike the ground first. To avoid these problems, check that the bottom edge of the club is level with the ground at address. Then hit a few shots. If the lie angle is correct, the start of the divot-mark will be uniform in shape and depth, and pointing at the target. If the lie angle is either too flat or too upright, check your set-up. If this is alright, the club professional can adjust the lie angle.

CORRECT LIE ANGLE

LIE ANGLE TOO FLAT

LIE ANGLE TOO UPRIGHT

Fairway woods

You should consider the same factors when buying a fairway wood that you do when purchasing a driver. However, the clubhead should be smaller because on the fairway it is more difficult to strike the ball out of the sweet spot of a big clubhead. Your main concern should be the club loft. A loft of between 15 and 18 degrees strikes a balance between distance and accuracy. It is also a good idea to introduce a utility wood, a type of fairway wood, to your set. These versatile clubs are effective from a variety of lies.

WOODS AND HYBRIDS: LOFT AND AVERAGE DISTANCE		
CLUB NUMBER	LOFT	DISTANCE
Driver	7–11°	220m (240yd)
3-wood	15°	200m (220yd)
5-wood	21°	175m (190yd)
2-hybrid	18°	190m (210yd)
3-hybrid	21°	175m (190yd)
4-hybrid	24°	165m (180yd)
5-hybrid	27°	155m (170yd)
6-hybrid	30°	145m (160yd)

Hybrids

The hybrid or rescue club has a smaller clubhead than that of a fairway wood. The clubhead is like an over-size long-iron with a bulbous back edge, and it produces the ball-flight features of a long-iron without any of the hardships. The hybrid is very versatile. It's a superb club to use off the tee on tight par 4s – the generous loft and relatively short shaft optimize accuracy without much drain on distance. The rounded, compact clubhead makes light work of clingy rough, and rounded design redistributes the clubhead mass. This boosts the size of the sweet spot on the face and lowers its centre of gravity, which make it more forgiving.

HYBRID
Compact and forgiving, the hybrid is suitable for a wide range of shots. It is even used for chipping and around the greens.

Irons

As with drivers, iron clubs used to be subtle variations of what was basically the same theme. Nowadays, however, manufacturers are competitive and coming up with the latest innovation. This means that there is a wide variety of clubhead designs. However, the key issues when you come to buy are: how much forgiveness do you want, how important is it for you to be able to shape the ball through the air, and do you like the club appearance? You then narrow your options, making the buying process that much easier. When it comes to clubhead construction, there are two main types: blades and peripherally weighted irons.

Blades

These clubs, by far the most popular irons up until the late 1970s, have a forged clubhead and a plain shape. Although relatively unforgiving to off-centre strikes, blades produce a purer feel at impact and offer greater scope for shaping the ball through the air. Today, blades are still favoured by traditionalists and some professionals and accomplished amateurs.

BLADE
Providing the purest feel at impact, blades make it much easier to shape shots at will through the air.

IRONS: LOFT AND AVERAGE DISTANCE

IRON NUMBER	LOFT	DISTANCE
2-iron	18°	190m (210yd)
3-iron	22°	175m (190yd)
4-iron	26°	165m (180yd)
5-iron	30°	155m (170yd)
6-iron	34°	145m (160yd)
7-iron	38°	135m (150yd)
8-iron	42°	130m (140yd)
9-iron	44°	120m (130yd)

Peripherally weighted irons

Also known as "cavity backs", the peripherally weighted irons often have cast rather than forged clubheads and are designed to offer maximum forgiveness to off-centre hits. This is because they have more weight at the extremities of the clubhead. In addition to peripherally weighted cast clubs, there are now many "in-between" peripherally weighted irons available, which offer some of the benefits of bladed irons yet are still forgiving to off-centre strikes. Some of these irons, especially those used by many of today's professionals, are even designed to look very much like a blade.

PERIPHERALLY WEIGHTED IRON
Peripherally weighted irons are more forgiving to off-centre strikes but do not make it so easy to shape shots.

Wedges

You should have at least three wedges within 46 and 62 degrees of loft for versatility in your short game. The degree of bounce you select depends on the kind of shots you wish to play. For fairway shots, less bounce is desirable (no more than 5 degrees). From most types of sand, soft ground, and rough, however, you need more bounce (between 10 and 14 degrees). Steel is the standard metal for wedge clubheads.

WEDGES: LOFT AND DISTANCE		
WEDGE TYPE	LOFT	DISTANCE
Pitching wedge	46°	100m (110yd)
Standard wedge	56°	75m (82yd)
Lob wedge	60°	55m (60yd)

SAND WEDGES
Clubs with lots of bounce work best in soft, powdery sand; clubs with less bounce are suited for coarser sand.

Putters

Since about 40 per cent of the shots in an average round are putts, you must use a putter with which you feel confident. Putters can have standard-length or long handles, and there are three main types of putterhead – peripherally weighted, mallet-headed, and centre-shafted. Peripherally weighted putters are made using the same principle employed in peripherally weighted irons. A mallet-headed putter has a semi-circular head and offers the same benefits as a peripherally weighted one. Centre-shafted putters are less forgiving with off-centre hits than a peripherally weighted club.

TAKE YOUR PICK
One of the three basic putter designs is the mallet-headed putter.

Putterface inserts

Manufacturers have responded to golfers' quest for maximum feel on the greens by introducing the concept of face-inserts in putters. Some inserts are made from relatively soft rubber compounds, while others are built up from complex mixtures of metals. The idea behind these inserts is to promote a soft feel off the putterface to enhance control and give the ball a smooth roll. Some professionals have fat grips fitted to their putters. These reduce excessive wrist action during the stroke.

PERIPHERALLY WEIGHTED PUTTERS
In these clubs, the weight is positioned across the clubface to minimize performance loss caused by off-centre strikes.

Types of play and handicaps

This book covers most aspects of how to play golf and what equipment to use. Here we examine the multitude of competitive and friendly formats of the game. The most popular types of play seen on courses all over the world are discussed, as are a few that are sadly not played often enough. Additionally, a full and clear explanation is given of how handicaps work with each format.

Strokeplay

Most professional and amateur tournaments take place under the format known as strokeplay. In this form of the game, you simply record your score for each hole, and add up the total at the end of the round. The person with the lowest score wins. The total number of shots taken in strokeplay is known as the "gross score". In a tour event, this is the score that counts because professional players do not have a handicap. But at the club level, each player's handicap is deducted from the gross figure to produce a "net score", which in most amateur events decides the winner.

Stableford

This format works on the principle of awarding points for scores gained on each hole. An albatross is worth five points, an eagle four points, a birdie three points, a par two points, a bogey one point, and anything worse than a bogey scores no points at all. The person with the highest score at the end of the round wins. Stableford offers the full handicap allowance to competitors.

Matchplay singles

This format involves head-to-head competition. Individual holes are won, lost, or halved (whereby each player scores the same), and every hole contributes to the state of play of the match. For example, the player who wins the first hole is "one-up". If that player wins the next hole, he or she goes "two-up", and if he or she loses the next, the player is back to "one-up". If a hole is halved, the match score stays the same. The match is decided when a player is "up" by more holes than there are holes left to play. For example, if a player is four-up with three holes to play, this is known as victory by four and three. If the match is all square after 18 holes, a sudden death play-off ensues. The golfer with the lowest handicap gives strokes to his or her opponent, based on three-quarters of the difference between the two handicaps. For example, if Player A has a handicap of 4 and Player B has a handicap of 16, three-quarters of the difference (12) is 8. Therefore, Player B receives a stroke from his or her opponent on each of the holes with a stroke index of between 1 and 8.

HANDICAPS ALLOW GOLFERS OF DIFFERENT ABILITIES TO COMPETE **ON EQUAL TERMS**.

Fourball betterball

This is similar to matchplay singles, only the game is played in pairs. Each player in the two pairings plays his or her own ball and the lowest score from each pair on each hole is the one that counts. The method of keeping score, and how the handicaps work, is the same as in matchplay singles. Fourball betterball can also be applied to stableford but seldom to strokeplay.

Foursomes

This is another game played in pairs, but here each pairing shares just one ball. One player in each pair tees off on the odd-numbered holes, the other on the even-numbered holes. Thereafter, alternate shots are played with the same ball until the hole is completed. This format is applicable to matchplay, strokeplay, and stableford. In matchplay foursomes, the pair with the lowest combined handicap gives shots to the other two players based on three-eighths of the difference. For example, if Team A has a combined handicap of 10 and Team B has a combined handicap of 26, then 16 is the difference. Since three-eighths of 16 is 6, B receives a stroke on holes with a stroke index between 1 and 6.

Greensomes

This is a variation on the foursomes format, the difference being that both golfers in each pair tee off and then select the more favourable of the two drives. Then, alternate shots are played as in foursomes. The handicap calculations work in exactly the same way as with foursomes. Greensomes is also a popular stableford format.

Bogey

This almost-forgotten format is essentially a game against par. The course is your opponent, and the scoring system is based on holes won, lost, or halved (as in matchplay). The only difference is that the game is not over until the last hole has been completed. The aim when playing the bogey format is to finish as many holes "up" on the course as possible. As you play, you receive shots from the course, most commonly based on three-quarters of your handicap allowance. If you play with a handicap of 8, for example, the course gives you six shots. You receive these shots on the holes that have a stroke index between 1 and 6.

HOW IS A HANDICAP CALCULATED?

Handicaps allow golfers of different abilities to compete on equal terms. Gaining your first handicap is a straightforward process that involves playing usually three rounds on the same course. You then combine the scores and divide it by three to arrive at a figure that is relative to the standard scratch score (SSS) of the course. For example, if you play three rounds and score 86, 91, and 84, these figures are then totalled to make 261. This number is then divided by three (which makes 87). If the SSS of the course is 70, then you will be given a handicap of 17. The maximum handicap for men is 28 and for women the upper limit is 36.

Your handicap is then adjusted every time you play in a strokeplay competition. There are three possible scenarios. Firstly, you can shoot a score better than your handicap, which means your handicap will be lowered. Secondly, you can shoot a score that is the same as, or one–three strokes above, your handicap. This places you in a "buffer zone", wherein your handicap does not move up or down. This zone allows for a minor dip in form, which does not warrant an increase in your handicap. Finally, you can shoot a score that is more than three shots above your handicap, that places you beyond the buffer zone. In this situation, your handicap will increase.

The etiquette of golf

The term "etiquette" can bring to mind images of an overly regimented code of behaviour. Following good etiquette ensures that everyone on the course enjoys their round. There are two key areas of etiquette: how to look after the course and behaviour on the course.

Looking after the course

You must ensure that your impact on the course is minimal. While you will not usually take a divot on par-4 or par-5 tees, if you take a divot on a par-3 tee, use the sand-and-soil mix provided to fill the divot-mark. If there is no sand-and-soil mix, simply place the divot back in its hole.

ALWAYS REPLACE DIVOTS

A divot that is immediately placed back in its hole soon repairs itself. But if a divot is not replaced, it leaves an ugly scar, making the course look scrappy, and it is harder for the greenkeeper to repair the divot-mark. Therefore, before leaving the scene of every fairway shot, place the divot back in its hole, and tread it down firmly with the sole of your shoe.

REPLACE TURF

REPAIR JOB

REPAIR PITCH-MARKS

Pitch-marks on the green are unsightly and can deflect a ball on its way to the hole. Not every shot played on to a green will leave a pitch-mark, but those that do should be repaired the moment you set foot on the green. You can use a pitch-mark repairer, which is designed specifically for the job, or alternatively a wooden tee-peg will suffice (the plastic ones bend). The procedure is simple and takes only a few seconds. Stick the pointed end of your tee-peg, or the fork of your pitch-mark repairer, into the ground and gently ease the turf up. This will level the indentation. The pitch-mark will then "heal" within 24 hours, whereas an untended pitch-mark can take weeks to recover completely. A green dotted with pitch-marks is no fun to putt on.

LEAVE NO TRACE IN THE SAND

Once you have played your bunker shot, use the rake provided to smooth the sand (see box, p.118). If there is no rake, use the back of your sand wedge. cover your footprints and the trough left by the clubhead.

BE CAREFUL WITH THE FLAG

Do not throw the flag across the green, as it damages the putting surface. Lower it gently to the ground. If you hit a putt and the ball strikes a flag lying on the green, you receive a two-shot penalty. Ideally, place it on the apron of the green.

How to behave on the course

While looking after the course is an essential requirement of good etiquette, your on-course behaviour is equally important. Inconsiderate conduct during a round can take the shine off even the sunniest of days. However, if you adhere to the advice given below, you will not be guilty of ruining other players' enjoyment.

WAIT YOUR TURN

Honour on the tee – who plays first – is secured by the golfer with the lowest score on the previous hole. On the first tee, honour is decided by lots or the toss of a coin. Elsewhere on the hole, the golfer furthest from the hole plays first. In a strokeplay event you can elect to continue to putt out after your initial approach putt.

OUT OF SIGHT, OUT OF MIND

Stand 45 degrees behind and to the right of the golfer; and four or five paces away. Do not talk or practice swings.

BE A GOOD TIMEKEEPER

If you fear your ball might be lost, play a provisional ball. Then, if the original ball is lost, you do not have to walk back to the site of the stroke. If the ball you feared lost is not sighted, and there is a group behind you, call them through. If your ball disappears into the rough, watch where it comes to rest and

"spot mark" it with a distinguishing feature, such as a tree that is along the same line. On the green, before you begin putting, leave your golf bag on the side of the green closest to the next tee, to collect it on your way to the next hole. Do not mark your card on the green, as this can hold up the players behind you. Instead, it is better to do this on the next tee while waiting your turn to play.

ALWAYS SHOUT "FORE!"

If you hit a wayward shot that you think might endanger others, shout "fore!" loudly and without hesitation.

BE CAREFUL WHERE YOU TREAD

On the green, be aware of where your playing partners' balls have come to rest and avoid treading on the line of their putts. On a soft putting surface your feet can leave marks as these may affect the smooth roll of a ball. Even on a firm green it is courteous to avoid treading on the line of another golfer's putt.

Form the perfect grip

The grip is almost certainly the most important fundamental skill of golf. Many golfers take their grip for granted simply because it feels comfortable. The trouble is, comfortable doesn't necessarily mean correct: you may well have a fault in your grip and not realize it. Although a change of grip is bound to feel uncomfortable for a while, this period need not last long if you rehearse as often as possible. Waggle the club around to familiarize yourself with the new feelings: you will be amazed at how quickly the different hand positions start to feel comfortable. The dedication you show in these initial stages will stand you in good stead for many years to come. A sound grip promotes a neutral clubface position throughout your swing, eliminating the need to make compensations as you swing.

> " A GOOD GRIP ALLOWS YOUR WRISTS TO HINGE FREELY – AND THE BETTER YOUR WRIST ACTION, **THE BETTER YOU STRIKE THE BALL**. "

GRIP VARIATIONS

Over the last 100 years or so there have been three accepted grips: the baseball grip, the overlapping grip, and the interlocking grip. The baseball grip is ideal for young golfers or those who have arthritic problems in their hands. By far the most popular style is the overlapping grip, where the little finger of the right hand literally rides "piggyback" on the forefinger of the left hand. This method is favoured by players such as Nick Faldo and Ernie Els. A variation on this method is the interlocking grip, where the little finger of the right hand is entwined with the forefinger of the left.

BASEBALL GRIP

OVERLAPPING GRIP

INTERLOCKING GRIP

Right hand
Hold the butt-end of the club steady

Left hand
Lay the club diagonally across the palm of your left hand

1 Rest the club on the ground so that the clubface looks straight at the target. Bringing your left hand forward, place the club handle diagonally across your palm, running from the base of your index finger through the middle of the palm. Close your fingers around the club, making sure that your thumb sits to the right of the centre on the handle. You should be able to see two and a half of the knuckles of your left hand.

Left-hand "V"
Make sure that the left-hand "V" points towards your chin

2 The palm of your right hand should mirror the position of the clubface, in other words it should face the target. Start by holding your right hand flat against the club's grip. Then feed the club into your hand, along the base of your middle two fingers.

Right-hand "V"
Make sure that the right-hand "V" points towards your right shoulder

3 Close the fingers of your right hand around the grip. Since this is an overlapping grip (see box, opposite), the little finger of your right hand should overlap the left forefinger. Your right thumb should run diagonally down the side of the club's grip.

Take aim

If your aim is poor, this will affect not only each shot you play but also your long-term golfing prospects. This is because if you aim incorrectly, it takes a bad swing to hit the ball towards your target, which means that you will be constantly making poor swings in an attempt to strike the ball in the right direction. The good news, however, is that taking aim is extremely simple, but it does require constant checking.

1 To aim correctly, identify an intermediate target on a line directly between the ball and the target. Then aim the clubface at that mark. This process is called "spot marking". Once you have identified your mark that is on the ball-to-target line, such as an old divot-mark, make this the focus of your attention. Aim the clubface at the spot.

GRIP FIRST, THEN TAKE AIM

Placing the club behind the ball one-handed and then forming your grip is not a good idea – it is too easy to twist the clubface. It is, therefore, best to establish your grip and make sure that it is comfortable before you place the clubhead behind the ball. Only then should you aim at your intermediate target.

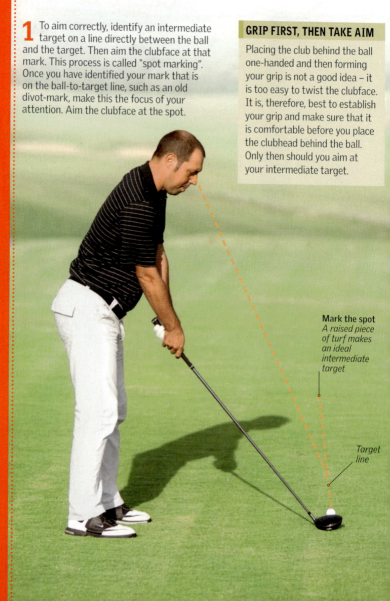

Mark the spot
A raised piece of turf makes an ideal intermediate target

Target line

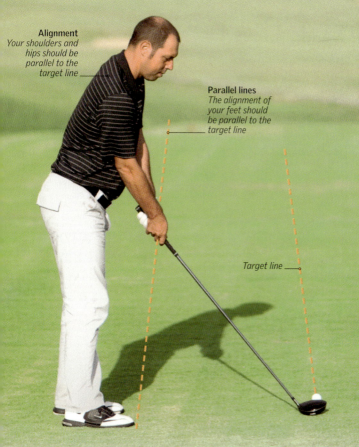

Alignment
Your shoulders and hips should be parallel to the target line

Parallel lines
The alignment of your feet should be parallel to the target line

Target line

2 Once the clubface is "spot marked", build the remaining elements of your stance around that position. If you want to hit a straight shot, your feet, hips, and shoulders should run parallel to the line along which the clubface is aiming. This position, known as perfect parallel alignment, improves your swing. When you are comfortable over the ball, focus on the intended target, look back at the ball, and then hit the shot.

PRACTISE WITH CLUBS ON THE GROUND

The practice ground is where you develop the "muscle memory" to make a good address position your second nature. Lay two clubs on the ground: one just outside the ball, and the other along the line of your toes. The outer club should point at the target – it serves as a reference to aim the clubface. The inner club should run parallel to the other club – it helps you align your feet. Keep your hips and shoulders parallel to the clubs on the ground.

AIM AND ALIGNMENT
Practising with two clubs on the ground helps you set up correctly.

Form the perfect stance

The stance is the aspect of your set-up that relates specifically to the width your feet are apart at address, and to the position of the ball relative to your feet. If you spread your feet the correct distance at address, you will benefit from a stable base, which enhances your balance and offers the mobility to make a powerful body-turn in your backswing. Apart from a good stance, correct ball position is also important. It helps ensure that the clubhead meets the ball on the ideal path and angle of attack. So make sure you follow these effective guidelines to establish the ideal stance.

MONITOR YOUR STANCE-WIDTH

It is simple to check the width of your stance which is a vital part of your set-up. Hold the butt-end of two clubs in each hand, and position one against your left shoulder and the other against your right. Let gravity take its course and note where each clubhead points. If your stance is the ideal width for the driver and long irons, the clubs will point at the inside of each of your heels.

> **THE WIDTH OF YOUR STANCE** IS VITAL FOR A CORRECT SET-UP.

1 Although your stance will change as you move through all the clubs in your bag (see box, above), it is good to first establish the correct stance when using a driver. Stand with your feet close together and the ball opposite your left heel. If your feet are close as you place the clubhead behind the ball, it is easier to see the ball in relation to your left foot.

Alignment
Practise with clubs on the ground in order to watch your alignment

Stance
Keep your feet close and the ball opposite your left heel

THE 3-CM (1¹/₄-IN) RULE DICTATES THE WIDTH OF YOUR STANCE

Hitting a driver requires the fullest, most dynamic swing of all the clubs in your bag – it is not surprising that your stance should be at its widest to offer maximum balance to support such a powerful movement. For the 3-iron through to the wedges, however, your stance should become progressively narrower, and the ball should gradually edge closer to the centre of your stance. Below are the three "benchmark" positions from which you can work out the ideal stance for all your irons.

3-IRON: Your feet should be 3cm (1¹/₄in) closer together than for the driver, and the ball should be 3cm (1¹/₄in) further away from your left instep. This ensures that the ball is positioned at the point where the clubhead reaches the bottom of its swing arc.

6-IRON: Your feet should be another 3cm (1¹/₄in) closer together, and the ball should also be 3cm (1¹/₄in) further away from your left instep.

9-IRON: With a 9-iron, your stance should narrow another 3cm (1¹/₄in), and the ball should again shift 3cm (1¹/₄in) back from your left instep.

This "3-cm" (1¹/₄in) rule should simplify the confusing questions of where to position the ball in your stance and how far apart to space your feet.

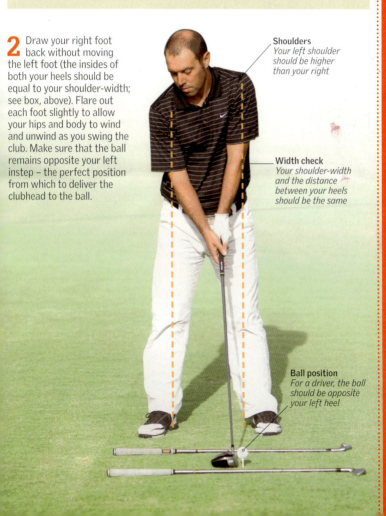

2 Draw your right foot back without moving the left foot (the insides of both your heels should be equal to your shoulder-width; see box, above). Flare out each foot slightly to allow your hips and body to wind and unwind as you swing the club. Make sure that the ball remains opposite your left instep – the perfect position from which to deliver the clubhead to the ball.

Shoulders
Your left shoulder should be higher than your right

Width check
Your shoulder-width and the distance between your heels should be the same

Ball position
For a driver, the ball should be opposite your left heel

Assume the right posture

Posture describes the angles in your legs and upper body at address and how you distribute your weight in the set-up. The key elements of a good posture are: the amount your upper body bends over from the waist; the amount of flex in your knees; and the distribution of your weight on each foot. Together, these factors influence the shape of your swing.

1 Grip a 5-iron normally (see pp.22–23), and spread your feet as if you were about to hit a proper shot (see pp.26–27). Then stand up straight, and with your hands just above the belt-height, extend the club out in front of you.

2 Bend over from your waist. Maintain the angle between your body and your arms. Keep bending until the clubhead rests on the ground.

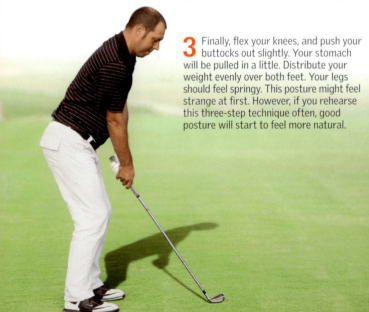

3 Finally, flex your knees, and push your buttocks out slightly. Your stomach will be pulled in a little. Distribute your weight evenly over both feet. Your legs should feel springy. This posture might feel strange at first. However, if you rehearse this three-step technique often, good posture will start to feel more natural.

Weight distribution

In an efficient golf swing, your weight shifts from your back foot in the backswing and to your front foot in the downswing to add power and provide balance. The ideal weight distribution, however, varies with every club. The driver, lofted woods, and long irons work best when you strike the ball with a sweeping blow. With the middle and short irons, your weight should be evenly spread, as this promotes the descending angle of attack. Unless you are manufacturing a stroke (see pp.156–59), your weight should not favour your front foot at address.

60% **40%**   **50%** **50%**

WOODS AND LONG IRONS
If 60 per cent of your weight favours your back foot, you can shift your weight behind the ball at the top of your backswing – crucial for striking the ball with a sweeping blow.

MIDDLE AND SHORT IRONS
For these shorter clubs, try to distribute your weight equally on each foot. This position promotes the correct angle of attack, which is slightly descending.

ONE HAND-SPAN SEPARATES HANDS FROM THIGHS

If you stand too far or too close to the ball you will struggle to hit it solidly. To avoid this, check how far your hands and the butt-end of the club are from the top of your thighs – you should see one hand-span of daylight. This suggests that you have enough room to swing your hands and arms freely, but not so much that you are reaching for the ball.

SPACE TO SWING
There should be one hand-span between the top of the grip and your thighs.

Identify the swing zones

Although a good golf swing is essentially a continuous, flowing movement, it is possible to break it down into key areas. When it comes to learning about your swing and improving your technique it is desirable to look at the swing in sections. This will help you understand how the swing works and why it is a chain reaction in which one good move often leads to another. It is therefore worthwhile familiarizing yourself with the key "swing zones".

 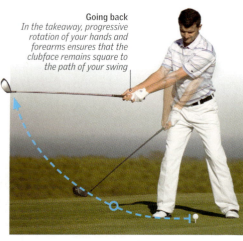

Going back
In the takeaway, progressive rotation of your hands and forearms ensures that the clubface remains square to the path of your swing

1 The set-up or address position determines both the shape and quality of your swing.

2 The first link in the swing-chain is the takeaway. This includes all that happens from when the club first moves away from the ball to the time when your hands are just beyond your right thigh. The takeaway is part of the backswing, but the latter refers to the swing-area where the clubhead is going from halfway back to the point just before the club starts down again.

3 The moment when you change direction from backswing to downswing is known as the transition. It is often the make-or-break time in terms of the quality of the shot.

" YOUR BODY WEIGHT MUST **MOVE IN HARMONY** WITH THE DIRECTION OF THE SWINGING CLUBHEAD. THIS **ADDS POWER** TO YOUR SHOTS. **"**

SWING PATHS

There are three basic swing paths through the hitting zone: inside-to-outside, outside-to-inside, and inside-to-square-to-inside. To hit a straight shot, inside-to-square-to-inside is the correct path, where the clubhead approaches the ball from inside the target line.

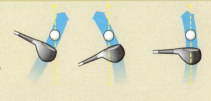

INSIDE-TO-OUTSIDE

OUTSIDE-TO-INSIDE

INSIDE-TO-SQUARE-TO-INSIDE

4 Just as the takeaway is part of the backswing, so the transition is part of the movement known as the downswing. Broadly speaking, downswing covers the area of the swing from when you start down to just before impact.

5 The hitting zone is the 30cm (12in) or so either side of impact, including the point where the clubhead meets the ball. The optimum swing path through the hitting zone is called "inside-to-square-to-inside"(see box, above).

6 A classic, balanced followthrough is the hallmark of a good player. You can use followthrough imagery to influence the shape of your swing and therefore control the flight and trajectory of your shots.

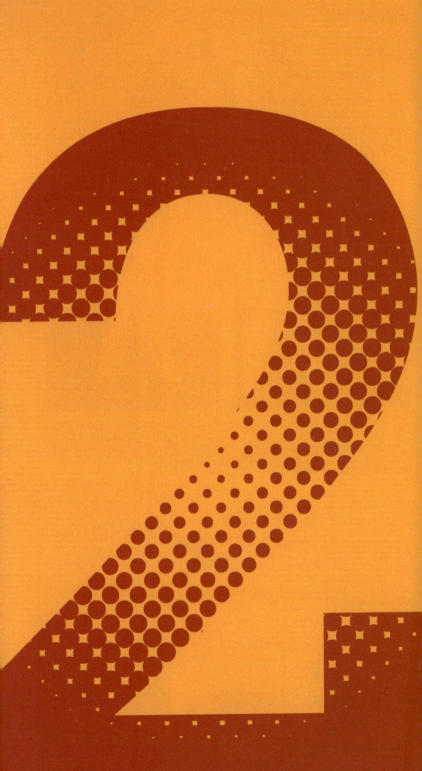

Driving and Iron Play

Off the tee

The driver is the most powerful club in your bag. Many golfers feel that they should try to hit their drive shots as hard as they can. However, position rather than power is the most important factor off the tee. Professional golfers hit most of their drives at only 70–80 per cent of full power. This is the kind of attitude you should apply to your tee-shot strategy: accuracy, not length, is paramount. Whenever you step on to the tee, you should not simply aim at the fairway in general but should instead identify a more specific target, such as a small mound or discoloured area of grass. This section of the book will help you hit consistently better tee shots, while the sequence below shows you how to make the perfect tee shot – as demonstrated by Rory McIlroy.

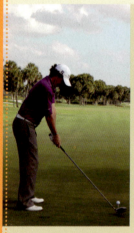

1 To form the perfect set-up, first flex your knees a little for a balanced stance. Your spine angle should be such that your arms hang down freely and there is a comfortable space between your hands and the tops of your thighs. Your toes, knees, hips, and shoulders should all run parallel to the target line, and the clubface should look directly at the target.

2 In your backswing, blend your body-turn and arm-swing, and make the appropriate wrist action to set the club on the perfect plane. Make sure your left shoulder turns under the chin.

3 At the top of your backswing, your hands should be above your right shoulder: a sure sign that the swing is on the correct plane. Also note the braced leg action in the image above.

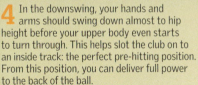

4 In the downswing, your hands and arms should swing down almost to hip height before your upper body even starts to turn through. This helps slot the club on to an inside track: the perfect pre-hitting position. From this position, you can deliver full power to the back of the ball.

5 By turning your left side, you can make room to swing the club into the ball on the correct path. As the clubhead swings through the hitting zone, the club moves back inside the target line, the perfect in-to-in swing path.

Step into a good stance

In your stance, the ideal distance between your feet is the same as the width of your shoulders (see pp.26–27). However, if you are especially tall and slim or have short legs, this rule might not apply. If either of these situations are applicable to you, then this fail-safe exercise, which is as easy as walking down the street, will help you establish the perfect base for your swing.

1 Take the longest club in your bag, your driver, and start walking as you would normally.

Plant your weight

Just as a boxer plants his or her weight on his back foot before delivering a knockout punch, so a golfer also needs to shift his or her weight in the same way to deliver maximum power to the ball. It is vital to transfer your weight on to your back foot at the top of your backswing. This is easier if you start your swing with your weight favouring your right side. Rehearse the given exercise to learn the mechanics of good weight distribution.

50%

" POSITIONING YOUR HEAD AND TORSO BEHIND THE BALL AT THE TOP OF YOUR BACKSWING GENERATES POWER. **"**

1 Stand upright, with your weight spread evenly over both feet. Assume your address position over the ball.

2 After a few paces, stop walking. It is important that you do not move your feet. This is your normal stride length, which provides optimum balance as you walk. This distance will also provide a good balance when you swing a golf club.

3 All you need to do now is turn and face the ball, making sure that your feet stay exactly the same distance apart.

60%

2 Tilt your spine angle away from the target so that 60 per cent of your weight is on your back foot.

TEE HEIGHT: THE 50 PER CENT RULE

Each driving club operates best when the ball is teed up at the correct height. However, as the size of driver heads varies greatly (and many people prefer to tee off with a lofted wood – see box, p.47), the ideal tee height should not be taken for granted.

To guarantee that the ball is always teed at the correct height, no matter what club you are using, make sure that 50 per cent of the ball is visible above the top edge of the clubface.

This practice is important because to strike driving shots solidly you need to swing the clubhead into the ball on a shallow angle of attack, sweeping the ball away with a level blow. You cannot do this if the ball is teed at the incorrect height. Teeing the ball too low means you may hit down steeply into impact; too high and you run the risk of hitting the ball on the upswing.

CENTRAL LINE
Whatever the size of clubhead, establish a tee height where the top edge of the clubface sits level with the middle of the ball.

Close the clubface at address

There are plenty of situations where it is advantageous to get the ball to run more than normal, such as when you are playing into a strong wind and need to generate maximum distance off the tee. Rehearse this drill on the practice ground for better results.

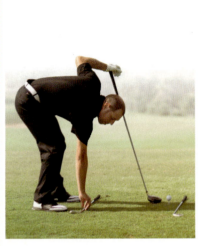

1 Place two clubs on the ground: one parallel with the ball-to-target line, and another pointing slightly right to establish a fractionally closed stance.

2 Rest the clubhead behind the ball, but do not apply your grip.

Good aim
This club points at the target

NORMAL CLUBFACE POSITION

CLUBFACE SLIGHTLY CLOSED

3 Keeping the clubhead behind the ball, use your right thumb and forefinger to twist the clubface 1cm (³/₈in) anti-clockwise. Making sure that you do not upset the new position of the clubface, carefully form your grip as you would normally.

Swing through the tee pegs

The purpose of this drill is to establish whether you swing the clubhead on the right path into and through impact. The correct swing path is vital to your chances of producing an accurate shot, as it eliminates sidespin, which causes the ball to curve in the air.

1 Line up a corridor of tee-pegs the width of two clubheads apart. Place one tee-peg in the middle.

2 Swing the club freely through this corridor. The clubhead should clip the lone tee-peg as it swings through. If the clubhead touches either line of the tee-pegs, you are swinging on the wrong lines.

3 When you are able to swing the clubhead cleanly, recreate the swing with a ball on the tee-peg.

Keep it all together

If you lose synchronization between your arm-swing and your body-turn at the start of your swing, it is difficult to regain it in the split-second it takes to reach the hitting stage. Here is an exercise to fix this problem.

Grip
Hold the club by the shaft

1 Take your driver and assume your normal stance. Feed the club up through your fingers so that the butt-end of the club rests at your navel and your hands grip the metal of the shaft.

2 Rehearse a backswing movement, turning your body and moving the club away from where the ball would normally be, but focus on keeping the butt-end of the club resting against your midriff. Go no further back than the point where your hands reach just beyond your right thigh. Repeat this movement over and over.

Feel a "Turn and a Swish" for a natural swing

There are two key elements of a perfect swing: body-turn and arm-swing. Too much of one and not enough of the other is disastrous – you will struggle to deliver the clubhead to the back of the ball on anything like the correct path or angle of attack. Too much arm-swing is a common problem, resulting from the shoulders not turning enough. This drill provides a constructive remedy.

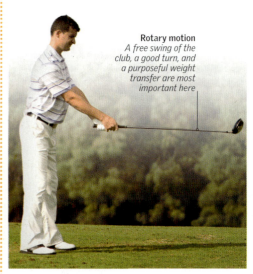

Rotary motion
A free swing of the club, a good turn, and a purposeful weight transfer are most important here

1 Stand with your arms stretched out. Swing the club around yourself, focus on your upper body motion, and let your arms swish the clubhead. As you make the return swing from right to left, your weight shifts towards the target and on to your left side.

2 Stand over a ball and bend until the clubhead is 60cm (2ft) above the ground. Make the same swing again.

3 Bend further from the waist until the clubhead rests on the ground and flex your knees. As you swing, repeat the sensations that you experienced in the previous steps – a full turn of the body, good weight transfer, and a free swish of the clubhead as you accelerate down and through the hitting area.

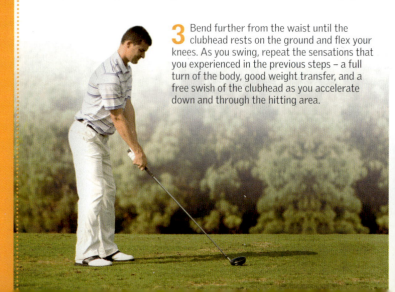

Shake hands with your target

A good release of the clubhead through impact (see p.31) is part of a powerful swing. It indicates that the club has been swung freely and with maximum clubhead speed. However, instead of releasing the clubhead, some amateur golfers attempt to guide the club or prod at the ball. This drill ensures that this key move is performed correctly.

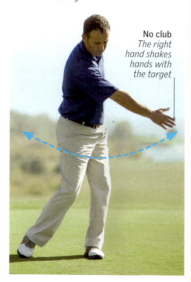

No club
The right hand shakes hands with the target

1 Adopt your normal posture but without a club in your hands. Let your right arm hang naturally, but put your left hand in your pocket.

2 Make half-swing movements (to hip-height on either side of the swing) with your right arm. Feel that you are "shaking hands" with the target as you swing your arm through the hitting zone.

3 Now rehearse a few practice swings with your driver. Swing in slow motion, and freeze when your right arm reaches horizontal with the ground in your followthrough. Your right hand should be in line with the target, ready to shake hands.

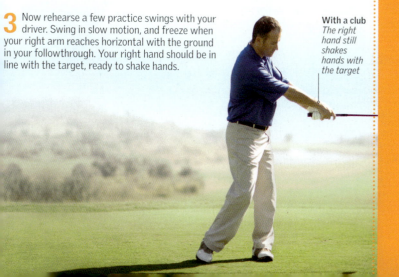

With a club
The right hand still shakes hands with the target

Turn your back on the target to generate power

Go low and slow: that is a great way to start your backswing with a driver. But where do you go from here? This exercise is very useful for anyone who lacks direction in the backswing, or is simply struggling with driving. It involves two key ideas, which together can have a great influence on the quality of your driving.

1 As you make your backswing, try to turn your back on the target. This will encourage you to make a full turn of your shoulders, will promote a much better weight transfer on to your right side, and will also help you set the club on the correct line at the top of your backswing.

2 When you reach the top of your backswing, try to point the club at the target. This idea is particularly beneficial for golfers who slice the majority of their drives. This is because these players tend to point the club to the left of the target, which results in an outside-the-line downswing (see p.31), causing them to cut across the ball through impact and produce a sliced drive.

COACHING TIP

Turning your back on the target ensures a good body rotation, which is essential for generating power, while pointing the club at the target means that the club will be on line. These two key elements combine to put you in a better position to swing the club down freely and on the correct swing path through impact, resulting in more clubhead speed and a more solid contact.

Synchronize your arm-swing with your body-turn

Losing coordination between your arm-swing and body-turn is a common fault. It can cause a loss of rhythm and make your swing feel ungainly. When this happens, even well-struck shots lack zip. With most golfers, the body moves too early and races ahead of the hand-and-arm action (the opposite problem is unusual). This is one of the main causes of a sliced drive: the shoulders and upper body unwind too fast in the downswing, throwing the hands and arms outside the ideal swing plane, causing the clubhead to cut across the ball from out to in. If you are slicing your drives, try this drill.

Backswing
Swing the club to the top as normal

Body position
Think of your hands and arms swinging down to hip height before your body starts to unwind

1 Take your driver and make a normal backswing. From the top of your backswing, concentrate on getting your hands and arms swinging the club down to hip height before your shoulders and upper body even start to unwind.

2 As you continue swinging downwards, your body should start to unwind in harmony with your hands and arms.

COACHING TIP

This drill eliminates the tendency for your shoulders to spin out too early in the downswing, which throws the club outside the correct path and causes a sliced drive. Improved synchronization will lead to better timing and more powerful ball striking.

Practise a pause

When using the driver, golfers tend to be aggressive when moving from the backswing to the downswing. This wrecks any chance of a solid strike. If you find yourself unable to shake this habit, this exercise will help.

"Lazy" downswing
The first movement down must not be rushed

1 Start by making a normal backswing, all the way to the top. Pause at this point for no more than a fraction of a second.

2 As you begin your downswing, cultivate a "lazy" feeling, as if this movement down is little more than the result of gravity.

Lift your heel for a fuller turn

For golfers who lack flexibility in the swing and struggle to make a full turn, lifting the left heel should give you an advantage. It enables you to make a more complete turn in the backswing, adding length to your swing and power to your shots.

1 Start your backswing as normal. When you reach the position in your backswing where you feel your hips and shoulders will not "give" any more, this is the point when the left heel is effectively pulled off the ground to release the right side and to allow for a bigger turn.

Turn your left shoulder

All kinds of mental imagery can help you produce a better swing. Here is an exercise to ensure that you make a 90-degree turn in your backswing, which is a minimum requirement for generating power with your driver.

Shoulder position
The left shoulder is now positioned roughly where the right shoulder was at address

1 Assume your normal address position, but think about the position of your right shoulder.

2 At the top of your backswing, turn your left shoulder into the position of the right shoulder at address. This transfers your weight on to the right side and makes for a good swing.

2 To initiate your downswing, plant your heel back on the ground. This allows your weight to move in the right direction – flowing towards the target.

Choke down on your driver

Too many golfers are obsessed with hitting the ball as far as possible. Yet most players would drive the ball a lot straighter and further, if they thought of the driver as a positional club. This drill will teach you how to hit your drives straighter, with no sacrifice in terms of distance.

1 Take your driver, and adopt your normal grip and address position.

2 Alter your grip so that your hands are 3–4cm (1^1/$_4$–1^1/$_2$in) nearer the clubhead and you can see the end of the club's grip protruding above your left hand. This is described as "choking down" on the club.

Create a box at the top of your swing

At the top of your backswing, the relationship between your right arm, hands, club shaft and upper body is an important one. This drill will help ensure that you are in the ideal position from which to start your downswing.

"THE ANGLE AT THE TOP OF THE BACKSWING SHOULD BE 90 DEGREES."

Grip
Choke down so that 3–4cm (1¼–1½in) of the club's grip protrudes above your left hand

Shoulder
Move your left shoulder under your chin to promote a full turn in the backswing

3 Swing normally: you should feel greater control. Although you have shortened the length of the club's shaft, thus reducing the arc and swing length, do not feel like you are making changes to your swing.

A 3-WOOD OFFERS MORE LOFT

Many golfers assume that the driver gives the most distance off the tee. However, this is not the case. The driver is a straight-faced club, and so sends the ball on a low trajectory. If you do not generate sufficient clubhead speed through impact, the ball will not achieve a decent length. If this is the case, it is better to use a 3-wood, which sends the ball on a higher trajectory, creating a longer drive. Another reason to use a 3-wood is if you have a fault in your swing that means you do not deliver a square blow to the back of the ball. In this situation, the driver's straight face will create lots of sidespin on the ball, which means losing distance as the shot curves through the air. Extra loft on a 3-wood's clubface helps to nullify this sidespin.

DRIVER VERSUS 3-WOOD
The clubface of a 3-wood (left) has more loft than the clubface of a driver (right). This makes a 3-wood easier to hit straight.

1 Swing your driver to the top and freeze right there. Now look over your right shoulder. You should see the shaft of the club forming a right angle with your right forearm, which in turn forms a right angle with your right upper arm, so that you have three sides of a box. This position encompasses the correct amount of wrist hinge.

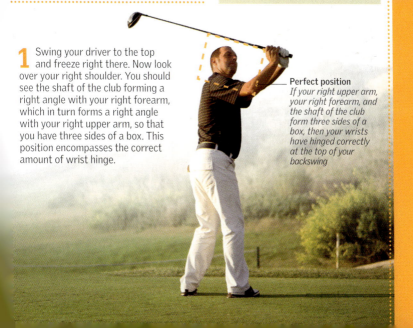

Perfect position
If your right upper arm, your right forearm, and the shaft of the club form three sides of a box, then your wrists have hinged correctly at the top of your backswing

If you slice, strengthen your grip

How you grip the club determines how the clubface strikes the ball. If your grip is weak – where the Vs formed by the thumb and forefinger (see pp.22–23) point towards your chin – it is unlikely that the clubface will be square with the ball at the point of impact. In most cases, the face will instead be open, leading to a glancing blow and a weak (often sliced) drive.

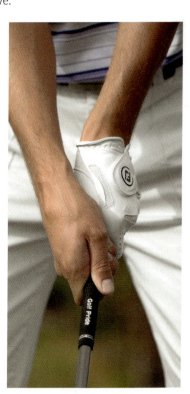

1 Grip your driver normally. Take your right hand off the club so that you have a clear view of your left hand. To steady the club, hold the bottom of the club's grip with your right hand. Loosen your left-hand grip to help you rotate your grip to the right until you see three knuckles on the back of your left hand. Your left thumb should sit slightly to the right of centre on the grip, and point straight down. The V formed by your left thumb and forefinger should now be pointing at your right shoulder.

2 Apply your right hand to the club's grip so that the V points at your right shoulder. You should be able to see just one knuckle on your right hand and three knuckles on the left hand.

COACHING TIP

Strengthening your grip ensures that the clubface is square at impact (for more solid strikes). This should eliminate sliced drives. Your new grip will also feel more powerful than your old grip. A stronger grip is of benefit to anyone struggling to generate sufficient distance off the tee.

If you hook, bring your grip back to neutral

The way you place your hands on the club's grip controls the behaviour of the clubface during your swing. If you are plagued by a persistent hook, your grip might be too strong, which means the clubface will be closed at impact. One of the best ways to cure a hook is to weaken an overly strong grip to make it neutral. This will help you deliver the clubface square to the back of the ball.

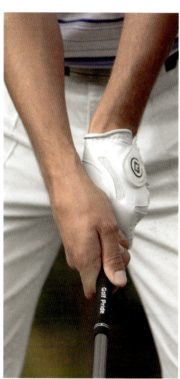

1 Form your grip on the driver as if you were about to hit a tee shot. Remove your right hand from the club. If your grip is too strong, you will probably see four knuckles on your left hand. Hold the bottom of the club's grip firmly with your right hand. Carefully rotate your left-hand grip to the left, so that you can see two or two-and-a-half knuckles on the back of your left hand.

2 Introduce your right hand so that it sits on top of the grip. You should now be able to see two knuckles on your right hand. Your right thumb should sit more on top of the grip, rather than to the right.

" AS YOU **FAMILIARIZE YOURSELF WITH THE HAND POSITIONS**, THE CLUBFACE WILL STAY NEUTRAL, MAKING IT EASIER TO HIT **STRAIGHT TEE SHOTS**. **"**

Iron play

Iron clubs are the precision tools in your bag, each one designed to hit the ball a certain distance. Iron play as a whole encompasses two types of shot: advancement shots, where on a long hole you play for position (in order to make the next stroke easier); and scoring shots, where the flag is the focus of your attention. Whichever shot you look at, trajectory and distance are the primary considerations.

This section of the book will teach you all the skills you need to improve the quality of your ball-striking with each iron, while the sequence below will show you how to make the perfect iron shot – as demonstrated by Tiger Woods.

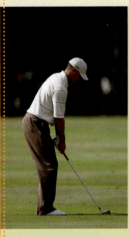  

1 For a perfect iron shot, maintain a good posture, as this will promote the correct action. This is because the angles established at address to a large degree determine the shape of the swing. Your alignment should also be perfect; your feet, hips, and shoulders should be parallel to one another. This promotes an on-line swing path.

2 Now complete the body turn, so that your wrists hinge fully and correctly. For this, you need to maintain a perfect plane, whereby the body pivot combined with an appropriate hand-and-arm swing produces a backswing that is on the ideal plane. Here the club does not quite reach horizontal at the top of your backswing.

3 As you approach impact, the angle of your spine should retain its original angle as it was at address. Maintaining this angle means that you do not need to make any significant height adjustments mid-swing to return the clubface to the ball. It is then a free and uninhibited swish through the hitting area.

4 Give yourself plenty of room to swing the club freely into and through impact on the correct path. This is facilitated by the action of your left side clearing out of the way quite early in your downswing. If your left side fails to clear, your arms and the club will become trapped too far on the inside.

5 Finally, swing the club within your physical limitations. Whether you are using a 3-iron or a 9-iron, the rhythm of the swing must stay the same. A perfectly balanced followthrough is the ideal sign-off for a controlled golf swing.

Establish good ball position for all your irons

Correct ball position in iron play is important, as it partly determines whether the clubhead will meet the ball at impact on the correct angle of attack. Obviously, there are many different numbered irons, and therefore ball position varies as you move through the clubs in your bag. This exercise will help you appreciate the correct positioning required for each iron.

1 Stand as if you were about to hit a long iron shot, with your feet comfortably spaced for good balance. Take a 3-iron, a 6-iron, a 9-iron, and three balls. Place one ball opposite yourself, on an imaginary line 3cm (1¼in) inside your left heel. Rest the clubhead of your 3-iron behind the ball. Position the second ball 3cm (1¼in) further back, and rest the 6-iron behind that. Finally, place the third ball 3cm (1¼in) still further back, and rest the 9-iron behind that. These three balls indicate the ideal positions for the clubs that you are holding.

COACHING TIP

Obviously there are more than three clubs in your set. But this all-in-one stance establishes some benchmark positions from which you can gauge the ideal ball position for all your irons. Using these positions when you swing ensures that the clubhead will meet the ball cleanly and on the correct angle of attack (see box, p.56).

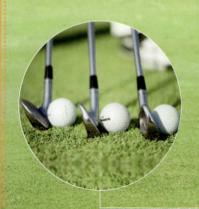

Stay square in the takeaway

As you make your backswing, the clubface should stay square to the path of your swing. Otherwise, you will be compelled to make compensations mid-swing in order to present the clubface square to the ball at the point of impact (which is vital for a straight shot). You should therefore check the position of the clubface in your swing, using this simple drill.

1 Make your normal takeaway. Stop when your hands are just above your right thigh. Compare the position of your clubface with the images below. In the correct position (main picture), the clubface looks to the right of the ball.

CLOSED CLUBFACE
The clubface is looking at the ball, which may result in a pull or hook.

OPEN CLUBFACE
The clubface is looking too far right, which may lead to a push or slice.

Square face
In the takeaway, the clubface must be square to the path of your swing

Move your head during the backswing

This drill, which requires a helper, enables you to determine exactly how much your head moves during your backswing. It is an especially revealing exercise for any golfers who believe the false assumption that the head should remain completely still throughout the swing.

1 Address the ball normally, and position a helper opposite you. Instruct the helper to dangle a club vertically in front of him- or herself so that as the helper looks at you, your head is bisected by the shaft. The helper can now monitor your head movement as you swing.

Let heel-toe-weighting teach you good balance

How you balance your weight at address has a much greater influence on the shape of your swing than you might think. This simple exercise will help you appreciate the relationship between weight distribution and how you swing an iron. It involves addressing a ball with the two extremes of poor weight distribution, so that you can then split the difference and find a happy medium.

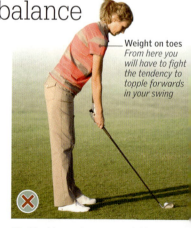

Weight on toes
From here you will have to fight the tendency to topple forwards in your swing

1 At address, place your weight on your toes, and swing. You will tend to lift yourself up and backwards to stop you falling forwards. To compensate for this extra height you have to dip to reach the ball. This makes your swing unbalanced.

2 Your head should move to the left of the helper's dangling club as your weight shifts on to your right side. Any other head position means that your weight is not moving correctly.

3 If necessary, repeat steps 1–2 until your helper confirms that your head has moved sufficiently to the left of the dangling shaft during your backswing.

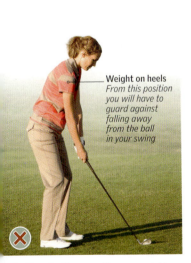

Weight on heels
From this position you will have to guard against falling away from the ball in your swing

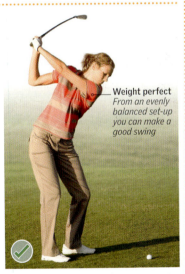

Weight perfect
From an evenly balanced set-up you can make a good swing

2 Now for the opposite: your weight should be on your heels. In this situation, the tendency is to stand too tall at address. Subconsciously you will dip your head and body in the backswing, and ultimately fall back on to your heels.

3 Now try to spread your weight evenly between your heels and toes. This is the perfect balance required for a good swing.

Find better direction with an intermediate target

In order to find the target, the ball must start on the correct line. Although this sounds obvious, many golfers tend to be obsessed with thinking about the last part of a ball's journey to the flag, when instead they might be better off considering the initial portion of the ball's flight. This drill requires only a small bucket (or similar object) to improve the initial direction of your shots.

1 Place a ball-bucket about 5m (5½yd) in front of you, along the ball-to-target line. Before you hit a shot, aim the clubface directly at the bucket .

WHEN AND WHY YOU TAKE A DIVOT

Some iron shots produce a divot and others do not. With more lofted clubs, good contact demands a progressively more descending angle of attack. With the 6-iron, for example, where the ball is positioned slightly further back in your stance (see p.52), the clubhead will meet the ball on a more downward path. Thus, the clubhead should first strike the ball and then the turf. The more lofted the club, the further back in your stance the ball is placed, and the larger the divot taken. Taking no divot at all is fine with longer irons, but no divot with clubs from the 5-iron upwards means that you are not striking the ball correctly. Refer to pp.78–79 to learn about your swing by examining your divot-mark.

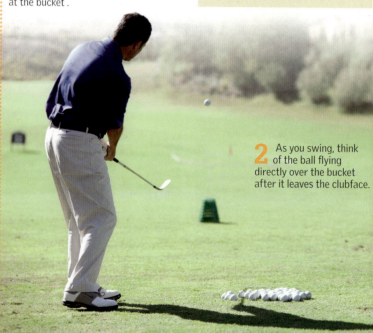

2 As you swing, think of the ball flying directly over the bucket after it leaves the clubface.

Learn about trajectory by examining the launch angle

The trajectory of a shot in the first 18m (20yd) or so of its flight is the ball's launch angle. It is a distance traversed so quickly that your head usually does not come up in time for you to see where the ball is going. However, establishing the launch angle for each iron is crucial as it enables you to make informed club selections.

1 Find a spot on the course for hitting shots so that there are overhanging branches between you and the target. Drop 12 balls about 18m (20yd) behind the branches.

❝ ESTABLISHING THE **LAUNCH ANGLE** FOR YOUR IRONS HELPS YOU MAKE **GOOD CLUB SELECTIONS**. ❞

2 Select a long iron, a mid-iron, and a short iron, and hit the balls towards the target. Note which clubs send the ball under the branches and which do not.

Split the difference to find the ideal swing speed

Going to extremes in your game can often help you find the happy medium. The following practice drill, which is a good example of this theory, might just help you find the perfect balance between control and speed when you swing an iron.

1 Take a 6-iron and three golf balls. Hit the first ball with every ounce of strength you can muster.

2 Hit the second ball as if you want it to fly half the distance of the first. Swing as slowly and lazily as you can.

3 With the final ball, split the difference. Make a swing that is halfway between overly hard and ridiculously easy.

COACHING TIP

Once you have worked through this drill and found the happy medium – a perfect balance between control and power – it is a good idea to spend the next 10–15 minutes becoming as familiar as possible with the tempo of this swing. You will quickly discover that this is the kind of swing that will work most effectively for all of your iron shots.

Flex your knee to add resistance to your swing

For most golfers, keeping the right knee flexed throughout the backswing stops the hips from turning more than 45 degrees. This provides a point of resistance against which the upper body can "wind up". The following drill will help you focus on maintaining your right-knee flex.

1 Take any iron and assume your normal address position. Introduce the right amount of flex in your knees (see p.28) and take your left hand off the club.

2 Rehearse a backswing. As you do so, shift your weight on to your right leg, keeping the knee braced. Your head should be over your flexed right knee. Repeat several times, focusing on shifting your weight on to your right knee.

3 Now put both hands on the club and try to replicate the same feelings in your proper backswing. If your knee straightens in your backswing, you are probably reverse pivoting, where your weight moves on to the left side instead of the right. If your knee slides to the right you are probably swaying off the ball too much. These situations are to be avoided.

Use your shadow

This exercise tells you a lot about your swing. But it does require one vital ingredient: sunshine. You will be amazed at what you can learn from your shadow. However, this is a drill for practice swings rather than hitting shots, as it requires you to take your eyes off the ball.

1 With the sun at your back, take up an address position so that the ball is right in the middle of your shadow. Using a long iron, swing to the top of your backswing. Your shadow should move to your right, so that the ball is in direct sunlight. This indicates that your weight has moved on to your right side – essential for a successful backswing.

CHECK YOUR DOWNSWING SPEED

Bobby Jones, who dominated the game in the 1920s and 30s, was a guru of golf instruction. One of his tips was: start your downswing at the same speed as you began your backswing. This helps you avoid the tendency to rush the first move down, which will ruin any golf shot, and gives your hands, arms, club, and body plenty of time to work together.

2 With the sun still at your back, address the ball again. Have a helper place a club on the ground so that it sits on the top of your shadow's head. As you swing back, watch your shadow and see how your head behaves. In any good swing, the head always stays almost level, from address until impact.

Wait, then apply the hit

The transition from backswing to downswing is a critical phase in your swing. In the split second when you change direction, you have two choices: you can make a great first move down and successfully store the power in your swing, or you can rush it and forget about producing a good shot. This simple drill will ensure that your swing falls into the former category every time.

Firm hold
The club is held towards the top of the shaft

Wrist pressure
With the club held in position, there will be some resistance in your wrists

1 Make a normal backswing, but have a helper hold the clubhead in position at the top. Initiate your downswing by moving your weight on to your left side, unwinding your hips a little. With the helper holding the clubhead firmly in position, you should feel some pressure in your wrists, as the angle formed between your forearms and the club shaft becomes more acute.

2 Now make some practice swings and try to recreate the feelings experienced in step 1. Remember, as you change direction, you should feel that the clubhead lags behind for a fraction of a second.

❝ THIS VITAL MOVE FROM THE BACKSWING TO THE DOWNSWING STORES ENERGY IN YOUR SWING. ❞

Play shots with your feet together

The golf swing is a complex action consisting of separate moving parts working together. Nevertheless, it is possible to identify two core elements: arm-swing and body-turn. Arm-swing is often neglected, because many golfers tend to rely too much on the bigger muscles in the shoulders and torso. Rehearse this drill to ensure that your arms play an active role in your swing.

1 Take a 6-iron and address a ball with your feet about 15cm (6in) apart. Grip the club lightly.

2 Swish the ball away with a free-flowing swing of the club. Try to swing so that you feel that your arms are doing much more work than your body.

3 If you lose your balance, your body is doing too much and your arms too little. Keep trying until you do not lose balance.

COACHING TIP

It is a good idea to punctuate your practice sessions with spells of hitting 12 or so shots with your feet together. This will remind you of the role of your arms in your swing. It will also promote a free swing of the club through the hitting area, which adds speed to your swing just where it is needed most. If too much upper-body motion is a persistent problem, this tip is for you.

Hit shots with the ball above your feet

Swinging the club into the ball on an inside path (see pp.30–31) is one of the greatest challenges in golf: perhaps on a par with serving an ace in tennis. If you find most of your shots curve from left-to-right through the air, you are not swinging the clubhead into impact on the correct (inside) path. Rehearse this practice drill to help correct this problem and to give your swing a better shape.

1 Find a sloping lie on your home course that allows you to set up with the ball noticeably above the level of your feet, as much as 30cm (12in) if possible. Use a 6-iron to hit shots from this position. This immediately establishes a more rounded backswing and encourages a better body-turn.

2 When you have hit about 12 shots from this sloping lie, find a flat area of ground, and see if you can replicate the swing sensations experienced in step 1.

Let a rope teach you tricks

One of Britain's most respected teachers, Jim Christine, is a great advocate of the benefits of swinging a rope in practice. Although you might wonder how this could possibly help your game, after trying this drill you will realize that a humble length of rope can improve the rhythm and efficiency of your swing, enabling you to create more clubhead speed with less effort. A worthwhile exercise, then.

1 Find a length of rope about 90cm (3ft) long. Assume your normal grip and address position.

2 Swing your arms upwards in tandem with your upper-body turn. The rope should curl gently around your shoulder.

3 When you slowly start to swing down, building up speed, the rope will catch up with you and "snap" in the hitting zone.

❝ PRACTISING WITH A ROPE IMPROVES THE RHYTHM OF YOUR SWING AND CREATES SPEED. ❞

Squeeze your elbows

This drill is based on the concept of developing better synchronization in your swing to ensure that your moving parts operate as a team, rather than independent of one another. This exercise examines the relationship between your arm-swing and body-turn in your backswing, which often becomes a little disjointed.

1 Trap a football, or similar sized and shaped object, between your elbows. Address a golf ball as you would normally.

Backswing
Stop when the club is horizontal with the ground

2 Now make a backswing, squeezing your elbows together to prevent the ball from falling.

Throw a football

This drill recreates the hand movements needed to release the clubhead through the hitting zone. The drill, which is performed outside, requires only a football.

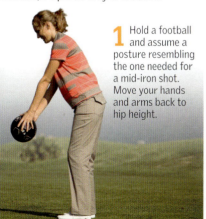

1 Hold a football and assume a posture resembling the one needed for a mid-iron shot. Move your hands and arms back to hip height.

2 Swing the ball through the hitting zone and spin it 30 degrees to the left of ball-to-target line. To achieve this, cross your right hand over your left in the impact zone. If the ball goes straight ahead of you, your club release will be incorrect.

Video yourself to learn about your set-up and swing

If you own or can borrow or hire a video camera, you have an excellent opportunity to examine and improve your swing. This drill focuses on a mid-iron swing, but you can also use a video camera to check aspects of your game covered in other parts of this book.

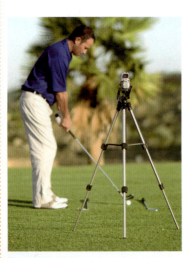
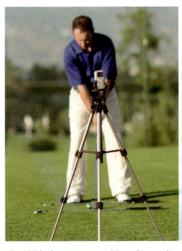

1 When checking your alignment, posture, and swing plane, the camera should point "down the line". Imagine a railway line in which the inner rail is on the line of your toes and the outer rail on ball-to-target line. The camera should be between these "rails", which you can mark with two clubs. To check ball position, stance, weight transfer, and followthrough, position the camera opposite you.

2 With the camera positioned opposite you, and with a mid-iron in your hand, begin filming. When you watch the video, check the width of your stance (see pp.26–27). Examine the ball position: it should be about two ball-widths inside your left heel. Ensure that your grip is neutral (see pp.22–23).

3 To check your alignment, move the camera to your right so that it looks "down the line". When you watch the video, check that your shoulders, hips, and toes run on a line parallel to the left of the flag, and the clubface aims at it. Check your posture.

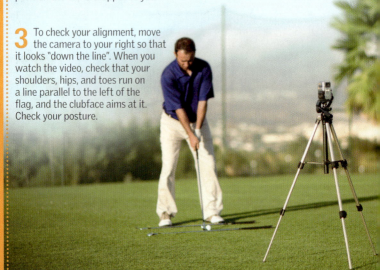

" WATCHING YOUR SWING ON VIDEO IS INCREDIBLY BENEFICIAL TO YOUR LONG-TERM PROGRESS. "

4 Now position the camera opposite you and make a few backswings. When you watch the video, check that your weight shifts on to your right foot and that your head moves laterally to the right (your left as you watch yourself) – 5–10cm (2–4in) is adequate.

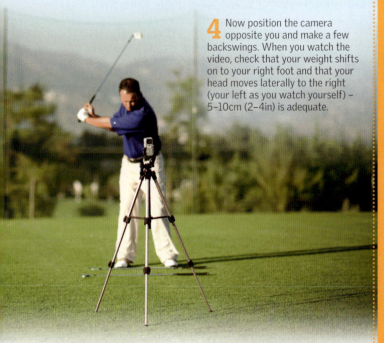

5 Position the camera "down the line". Rehearse a backswing, and freeze when your left arm is horizontal to the ground. If your wrists hinge correctly, the club sets on to the backswing plane, whereby the butt-end of the shaft points at a spot between the ball and your toes.

6 Now hit some shots. To check your downswing, freeze the video when your left arm is horizontal to the ground. To check your followthrough, position the camera opposite you, and hit some shots. When watching the video, check that your right shoulder is over your left foot.

Fairway techniques

Making a good decision on the tee, and hitting a solid drive is an important start. Once the tee shot is away, you then have to turn your attention to the second shot. If you are on a par 3, your second shot should be a putt, but on the longer holes, you will be aiming to hit the green or find a good position further up the fairway. As your game improves, you will realize that shooting a low score is not about all-out attack. Golf requires good judgement as well as great skill.

Turn par 5s into a three-part strategy

The key is to treat the hole as if it is in three parts. A length of around 180–200m (195–220yd) is adequate. Keep the ball in play and remember that, on all but the longest par 5, a controlled 180-m (195-yd) second shot will leave you with little more than a short-to-medium iron to the green. A birdie-putt is then one easy step away.

PLAN YOUR STRATEGY

Use a course planner to work out how you intend to play the hole. Rethink par 5 as a short series of mini-challenges. Put simply – divide and conquer.

Avoid "sucker" pin placements

A typical example of a sucker pin placement is a pin on the right-hand edge of the green closely guarded by a deep bunker to the right. Another is a pin at the front-edge of a green protected by water. In such situations, you only have to stray off-line by a few paces – not a terrible shot by any means – for the penalty to be severe. Do not be tempted into attacking the pin: whenever you see a sucker pin placement, aim for the centre of the green, giving yourself a comfortable margin for error.

AIM DEAD CENTRE

If, as here, the pin is placed close to a left-hand bunker, ignore the flag and aim for the centre of the green. A long putt is a better prospect than a tough bunker shot.

Observe a 10-pace rule in deep rough

If you cannot see the ball from 10 paces, you should pitch it safely into the middle of the fairway, where you will be back in control of your game. This reduces the chances of making a high score on the hole. If you go with a longer club and try to hit the green from a terrible lie, the odds are in favour of a mishit. The ball could go anywhere: since you have less control over the ball, you could end up in a bad spot.

A BAD LIE
When the ball is in deep rough, do not risk an overambitious recovery shot from the rough. When in doubt, play the simple option.

Add distance on the angle

Most course planners (course maps that indicate distances between the green and various points on the fairway for each hole) are measured from the middle of the fairway to the centre of the green. If you are in the rough, the angle effectively increases the distance to the centre of the green (as shown on the course planner) by as much as 5 per cent. A shot from 150m (165yd), for example, might gain an extra 7.5m (8yd). Also check the flag position. If it is central, you can rely on the number in the book. But if the flag is at the front or back of the green, add or subtract distance accordingly.

DO YOUR SUMS
Consult the course planner, and make the necessary alterations when working out the distance to the pin. This can make the difference between a short birdie-putt and a potential three-putt.

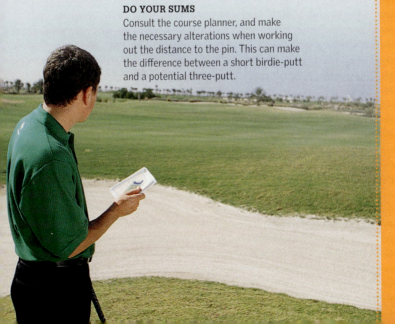

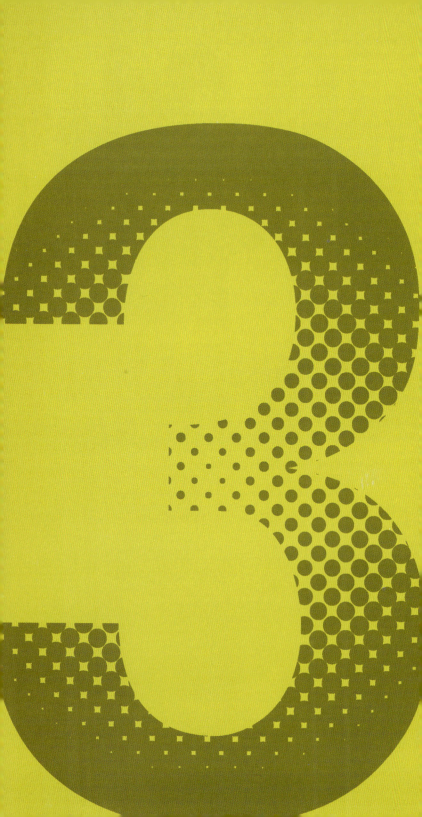

Approach Shots

Pitching

The pitching wedge comes into operation from 35m (38yd) to 110m (120yd) away from the green. From this position, a tour professional will land the ball close enough to the flag so that only one putt is required. Most amateurs, however, are just happy to hit the green. Even allowing for the remarkable skills of top tour players, this difference is too big. For one thing, distance is not an issue: you do not need to generate lots of power. Also, because a shorter swing is required, accuracy and control should be much more attainable.

This section of the book will provide you with all the necessary knowledge to familiarize you with the nuances in techniques that are unique to pitching, while the sequence below will show you how to make the perfect pitch shot – as demonstrated by Paul Casey.

1 Your address position should be perfectly square. Let your clubhead barely touch the ground. This helps remove tension from your hands and arms. It also facilitates a smooth move away from the ball.

2 Make sure your hand-and-arm swing works with your body pivot. As you turn your body, let your hands and arms follow. While this is happening, your wrists should hinge, setting the club on the perfect plane at the top. The lower half of your body should be stable, your knees flexed, and your hips resisting the turning motion of your torso.

3 Transfer your weight on to your left side, in the direction of the target. Your right shoulder should be tucked in to help deliver the club to the ball from an inside path of attack.

4 Let your body wind up as your hands and arms swing the club upwards in the backswing, so that your downswing is controlled by harmonizing the unwinding of your body with your arms and hands as they swing down and through impact. This smooth, controlled acceleration brings you into a wonderful impact position.

5 Your followthrough should be the same length as your backswing, as it helps produce smooth acceleration through the hitting zone. When professionals play this shot, the clean strike is what creates plenty of backspin on the ball. There is no need to hit the ball hard in order to achieve this; instead, improve your mechanics.

Open your stance

When playing most shots, perfect parallel alignment – where your toes, hips, and shoulders run along the same line – is required. However, pitch shots are unlike any other iron shot. To be a good pitcher your stance needs to be slightly open, and this drill will help you make the appropriate change.

1 Address the ball as you would to hit a normal iron shot, with your stance parallel to the target line. Place two irons on the ground to help you find perfect parallel alignment.

Keep your hands soft for a free-flowing swing

It only takes a little extra tightness in your grip for tension to spread into your arms and shoulders. This tends to lead to a poor first move away from the ball, and your whole swing will lack fluidity and rhythm. This is disastrous for a pitch shot.

Grip pressure
Hold the club lightly and keep your hands relaxed

1 Address the shot normally. Just before you take the club away from the ball, ease the grip pressure in your left hand by about 10 per cent. Use this pressure release as the trigger to start your backswing.

Open stance
Draw your left foot back approximately 5cm (2in)

❝ AN OPEN STANCE CREATES RESISTANCE IN YOUR LEGS AND HIPS, GIVING YOU CONTROL. ❞**

2 Now draw your left foot back about 5cm (2in) to open your stance. Keep your shoulders square, though. This element of your set-up must remain the same.

Check your swing plane halfway back

This drill uses the same "frozen" position employed in the drill on p.77. It will show you a simple way to check if your swing is on the correct plane in the backswing, which is vital to your chances of making a good swing.

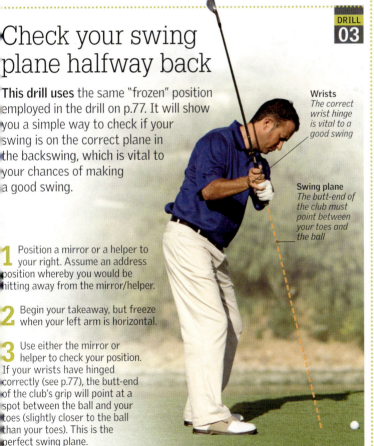

DRILL
03

Wrists
The correct wrist hinge is vital to a good swing

Swing plane
The butt-end of the club must point between your toes and the ball

1 Position a mirror or a helper to your right. Assume an address position whereby you would be hitting away from the mirror/helper.

2 Begin your takeaway, but freeze when your left arm is horizontal.

3 Use either the mirror or helper to check your position. If your wrists have hinged correctly (see p.77), the butt-end of the club's grip will point at a spot between the ball and your toes (slightly closer to the ball than your toes). This is the perfect swing plane.

Swing down on the path of your backswing

Sometimes the simplest of thoughts can clear your mind and clarify your swing objectives. With pitching, for example, it is easy to become so obsessed with hitting the target that you actually forget what you have to do in your swing. This simple drill will provide a clear swing thought that will improve your pitching.

❝ PERFORM A COUPLE OF 'DUMMY RUN' BACKSWINGS TO HELP ESTABLISH A STRONG VISUAL REFERENCE. ❞

Takeaway path
The clubhead forms a gradual arc inside

Downswing
Try to swing the club down on the same path it went back on

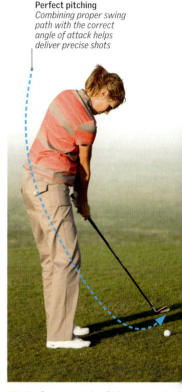

Perfect pitching
Combining proper swing path with the correct angle of attack helps deliver precise shots

1 As you start your swing, be conscious of your takeaway path. Ideally, the clubhead should move straight back for the first 30–45cm (12–18in) and then gradually arc inside in response to your body-turn (see pp.30–31).

2 Perform a couple of "dummy run" backswings to help establish a strong visual reference. Make it the sole objective in your downswing to swing the club into impact on exactly the same path that it went back on. Do not think about anything else.

Make a right angle in your backswing

Poor pitching is often the result of either too much wrist hinge in the backswing, where the hands pick the club up too abruptly; or too little wrist hinge, where the wrists remain stiff as the club swings back. Either situation damages your ball-striking because if you cannot set the club correctly in the backswing, you will never produce the ideal angle of attack into impact. This drill will ensure that the right wrist hinge takes place in your backswing – and at exactly the right time.

1 Take your pitching wedge and address the ball as normal. Begin your backswing, but freeze at the point where your left arm is horizontal. Compare your position in the three images shown here.

Right angle
The shaft of the club and the left forearm form a right angle

OBTUSE ANGLE
The angle between the left forearm and the club is too wide: the wrists have not hinged sufficiently.

ACUTE ANGLE
The wrists have done too much, and there is a poor body-turn. Try to get the club a little wider as you turn your upper body.

Check your divot marks

The divot-mark (or lack of one) you leave in the ground after a pitch shot can tell you a great deal about the shape and quality of your swing. Each divot-mark reveals the individual traits of your game. Knowing how to interpret your divot-mark can lead to clues as to how you can hit better pitch shots. Use the information in this drill to decode the information your divot-marks give you.

DEEP DIVOT-MARK

Deep divot-marks and erratic ball-striking suggest that your swing is narrow, causing you to swing the clubhead into impact on a steep angle of attack. This means you will be chopping down into the ground behind the ball. If these problems sound familiar, this drill will improve the quality of your ball-striking.

1 Make sure the ball is not close to or directly opposite your left heel, as this might cause you to hit behind the ball.

2 To shallow your angle of attack and start striking the ball more cleanly, try to delay hinging your wrists in your backswing.

NO DIVOT-MARK

Chances are that you are trying to help the ball into the air with a scooping motion if many of your shots leave no divot-mark at all, and you are also occasionally hitting heavy shots, where the ball flies barely half its proper distance. This indicates that the clubhead has travelled beyond the lowest point in its swing arc (see p.82).

1 Check that the ball is positioned correctly in the middle of your stance. This will help promote the required descending blow.

2 Examine the weight transfer in your swing. If you are hitting up on the ball, you are hanging back on your right side in the downswing. To solve this problem, let your weight flow on to your left as the club swings towards impact. With your weight travelling in the same direction as the club, you can hit down on the ball.

❝ KNOWING HOW TO INTERPRET YOUR DIVOT-MARK CAN LEAD TO CLUES AS TO HOW **YOU CAN HIT BETTER PITCH SHOTS**. ❞

Target line

Target line

DIVOT-MARK LEFT OF THE TARGET

When a pitch shot finishes left of the target, most probably the divot-mark will be pointing that way, too. This problem is caused by the clubhead approaching the ball from outside the correct line (see pp.30–31) and travelling to the left of the target through impact. But once you have effected the suggested changes, everything should be back on line.

1 Narrow your stance by 5cm (2in). This helps your arms to play an active role (see p.62), which encourages a correct swing path.

2 When you are at the top of your backswing, start down with your hands and arms. Try to feel that your downswing consists of more hand and arm swing and less body movement. This will enable you to swing the club into impact from slightly inside (see pp.30–31), which is ideal.

DIVOT-MARK RIGHT OF THE TARGET

A divot-mark pointing right of the target is not as common as one pointing to the left. This happens when your hips do not clear out of the way in the downswing and the clubhead gets trapped on the inside. This leads to an in-to-out swing path. At impact, the clubhead travels to the right and the ball flies to the right of the target.

1 Check that the ball is not nearer your right foot than your left foot. If it is so, open your stance so that your toe-to-toe line runs left of the target.

2 At the top of your backswing, initiate your downswing by turning your hips so that there is plenty of space for your hands and arms to swing on the correct path.

Think of distance, not direction

The essence of a good pitch shot is being able to see a target and make an appropriate length swing to produce the required amount of carry through the air. One of the biggest problems golfers have with their approach play is not knowing precisely how hard to hit shots of different distances. This drill provides you with this useful information.

1 Next time you are at the range and you want to work on your pitching, identify a specific target, whereby you know exactly how far it is from you. Do not aim at something beyond the distance you can comfortably hit with a wedge.

2 Hit pitch shots to this target, and judge every one in terms of distance. Whether the ball comes up short, long, or perfect will provide you with feedback you can use to make adjustments to the feel of your swing.

> " THE ESSENCE OF A GOOD PITCH SHOT IS TO MAKE AN **APPROPRIATE LENGTH SWING** TO PRODUCE THE **REQUIRED AMOUNT OF CARRY THROUGH THE AIR**. "

Swing around the clock to vary your distance

A pitch shot of a certain distance requires a length of backswing that helps you swing down and through the hitting zone with smooth acceleration (see p.88). You can determine the length for each distance by working through this drill. It requires you to make three different-length backswings based on the numbers on a clock face.

9 o'clock

1 Imagine the ball at 6 o'clock. Swing your arms back until they reach 9 o'clock, then accelerate into your downswing and through impact.

10 o'clock

2 With your next shot, stop your backswing when your hands reach 10 o'clock. Swing down as you did in step 1. Check the ball distance after each shot.

11 o'clock

3 Finally, make a swing in which your hands move all the way to 11 o'clock in your backswing.

THE GEOMETRY OF A PITCH SHOT

A good pitch shot requires a fairly steep angle of attack. To achieve this, check that your stance is slightly open, the ball is in the middle of your stance, and your wrists are set correctly in your backswing. It is only then that you will produce the downward blow that gives a clean contact and good backspin.

DIVOT-MARK
A descending angle of attack will automatically create a divot-mark.

Find the bottom of your swing for crisp strikes

Controlling the distance you hit your pitch shots is impossible, unless you learn to strike the ball consistently out of the clubhead's sweet spot. To do this, the ball must be positioned at the bottom of your swing arc – the point where the clubhead first comes into contact with the turf. Anywhere else in your stance, and you have to make unnatural compensations to avoid hitting the shot heavy or thin. This straightforward drill will help you locate the bottom of your swing arc and will confirm the ideal place to put the ball in your stance.

1 Stand in a closely mown area of grass and make a disciplined practice swing. Take care not to make a half-hearted swish, but a dynamic movement that closely resembles your actual swing.

Divot-mark
The beginning of the mark is the best place to position the ball

2 Note where the clubhead first comes into contact with the ground. This is the perfect place to position the ball in your stance.

Check ball position
Hit balls placed along a line that indicates the bottom of your swing. The divot-mark should start slightly in front of the line

Match your swing length to every pitch

If golf was an exact science you would be able to leave yourself with your ideal-distance pitch shot every time – and you would never hit a bad shot. But golf is not like that, and inevitably you have to play pitch shots from a variety of distances during a normal round. This is part of the game's charm and challenge. The following drill will improve your ability to match the correct swing to shots of different lengths. It will also help you establish your favourite pitching distance, which will make you better at seeing a certain length shot and matching the correct swing to it.

1 Arm yourself with a bag of balls and however many pitching clubs you have in your golf bag (you should have at least three: your pitching wedge, another slightly more lofted wedge, and your sand wedge).

2 Find a quiet green. Starting from about 35m (38yd) from the flag, drop a ball, move 5m (5$\frac{1}{2}$yd) back, drop another ball and so on. Stop when you are about 110m (120yd) from the green.

3 Starting with the shortest shot, work your way back from the target, pitching each ball towards the flag. As there are 5-m (5$\frac{1}{2}$-yd) gaps between each ball, you will have to alter your swing slightly for every shot. You may also want to go with progressively less loft as the shots become longer.

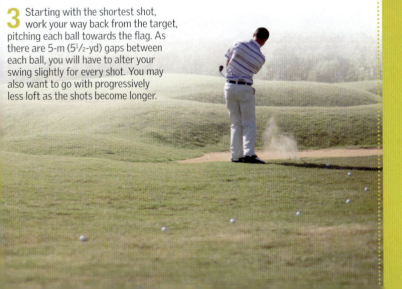

Free up your swing

If you struggle to get your swing off to a smooth start, this exercise might just release the tension in your swing and help you wield the club more freely. It also removes the tendency to hit at the ball too aggressively, which can cause problems in your swing.

1 Tee up five or six balls in a row, approximately 10cm (4in) apart.

2 Address the first ball in the line. For the purposes of this exercise, use either a pitching wedge or a 9-iron club.

Hover your club

If you are pitching from rough, it is easy for the clubhead to become snagged in the grass during your takeaway. You can prevent this from happening if you hover the clubhead behind the ball at address. This technique guarantees a smooth start to your swing.

1 Place a ball in light rough and address it normally with your pitching wedge, with the clubhead resting on the ground.

2 Raise the clubhead so that it is hovering in a position level with the ball's equator. But avoid lifting the club with your hands alone.

3 You are now in a good position to sweep the clubhead back freely.

COACHING TIP

At first you might struggle to hit every ball out of the middle of the clubface. But if you maintain an easy rhythm, after a couple of tries you will notice that your rhythm is smoother and more natural. Your swing will not be restricted by tension, and as a result you will start to feel what it is like to release the club more freely through the ball.

Once you are confident that these feelings are ingrained in your swing, try to replicate them when you hit pitch shots during a round.

3 Start with a half swing and build up gradually. From the time that you address the first ball, the clubhead should not stop moving until the last ball is sent.

Try right-armed swings

DRILL 13

With golf's shorter shots, you might want to guide the ball towards the target. However, your desire for accuracy will often lead to a missed green. To produce a good pitch shot, you have to release the club properly (see pp.30–31). This drill will help you achieve this.

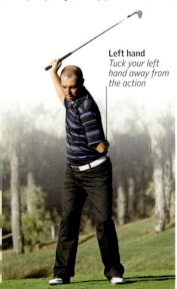

Left hand
Tuck your left hand away from the action

Downswing
Swing so the club is freewheeling through the hitting zone

1 Hold the club halfway down the grip with your right hand. Make a three-quarter-length backswing.

2 Swish the clubhead in your downswing so that the club is freewheeling through the hitting zone.

Hit the bucket for accuracy

It is easy to hit pitch shots on practice ground and be satisfied with a loose grouping in the distance. In reality, however, pitch shots need to be accurate. You should be looking to knock them close to the flag each time: merely hitting the green is not enough.

1 Place a bucket on the range, about 30m (33yd) away, as the target. From such a short distance, it is best to use your most lofted wedge.

2 Now hit a few pitch shots, and try to get the ball into the bucket (without the ball bouncing on the turf first). This forces you to be specific about your target.

Feel controlled aggression

Pitch shots are predominantly "touch" shots played from a distance, which means many golfers become a little tentative with the strike. You cannot afford to do this. Pitch shots are control shots, but they still need to be struck with authority. Here is a simple drill to help you make a more authoritative strike.

1 Take your pitching wedge and find a thick area of rough.

2 Make some smooth practice swings. Build up speed gradually in your downswing, and feel as if you are swishing the clubhead through the long grass. Be positive and get used to the feeling of the clubhead zipping through the hitting area.

Pre-set impact position

A slightly descending angle of attack is essential for accurate short-iron play (see box, p.81). This produces the right kind of strike – ball-then-turf – which in turn gives you control. Try this exercise to help promote the correct angle of attack.

Body
Open your hips and torso slightly at impact

Hands
Your hands should be ahead of the ball at impact

1 Pre-set your impact position by opening your hips slightly and lifting your right heel off the ground. Your hands should be ahead of the ball and the shaft must lean forwards.

2 Make your swing and try to return to the position created in step 1. It should be easier to replicate a good impact position because you started from a good impact position.

3 Once you have repeated step 2 a number of times, try hitting a few shots using this pre-setting technique.

SOFTER METALS PROVIDE MORE FEEL

All types of equipment are discussed on pp.14–17, but now is an apt time to consider a wedge with a metal compound clubface that gives you more feel around the green. A popular alternative to steel is beryllium-copper as it is softer than steel and allows you to gain more backspin on the ball.

Soft metal
Wedges with beryllium-copper heads are popular

FEEL THE CONTROL

Since the essence of a great short game is touch, you can only benefit from having a wedge featuring a soft-metal clubhead, as the ball comes off the face with more spin.

Think of gradual acceleration in the downswing

Mickey Wright, once referring to the need to build up clubhead speed gradually in the downswing, said: "You cannot start a car from a dead start and put it immediately up to 70 miles an hour." Although pitch shots are control shots, gradual acceleration is still required in the downswing to produce a proper strike.

Halfway down
The club should be gradually accelerating

1 Set up a shot at the practice range, and make what feels like a comfortable-length backswing with a pitching wedge.

2 Imagine your hands and club are rollercoaster cars, and the top of your backswing is the ride's highest point. The "cars" should slowly start their descent and gradually pick up speed. At the bottom of the ride, the clubhead should reach top speed.

COACHING TIP

In the hitting zone, your club should be moving at the optimum speed, while during the followthrough, your hands, arms, and club have to freewheel through to the finish of your swing.

HITTING ZONE   FOLLOWTHROUGH

Aim at multiple targets when you practise

When you play a round of golf, you only ever get one attempt at each shot. The pressure on your pitching is perhaps the greatest of all the shots, because you are aiming at the most well-protected area of the course where all manner of hazards, such as sand or water, guard the green. Work on this "multiple-target" drill in your practice sessions so that on the golf course you will be up to the challenge of hitting the right shot the first time.

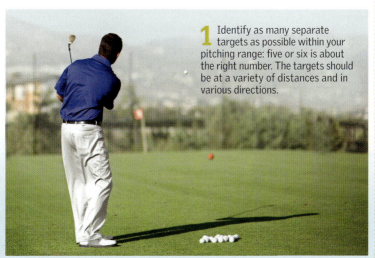

1 Identify as many separate targets as possible within your pitching range: five or six is about the right number. The targets should be at a variety of distances and in various directions.

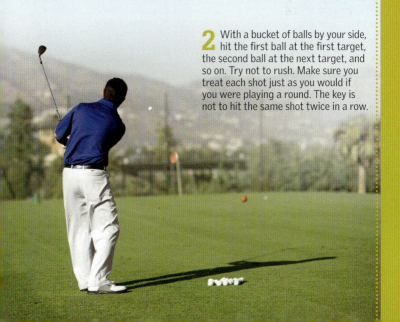

2 With a bucket of balls by your side, hit the first ball at the first target, the second ball at the next target, and so on. Try not to rush. Make sure you treat each shot just as you would if you were playing a round. The key is not to hit the same shot twice in a row.

Chipping

Even the best golfers in the world cannot find the green every time with their approach shots. They often miss the target numerous times in a round. A nicely played chip gives you an outside chance of a "chip-in" birdie, which will send you off to the next tee with a spring in your step. Even if you do not hole the shot, the ball should finish close to the hole. This takes the pressure off your putting – a significant factor when you are under pressure to produce a good score.

A proficient chipper must control the four key ingredients that combine to determine where the ball comes to rest on the green: height, carry, spin, and roll. Everything you read and do in this section is designed to give you the necessary skills to master these skills, while the sequence below shows you how to make the perfect chip shot – as demonstrated by Barry Lane.

1 Always remember the adage: ball back, hands and weight forward. This means that you should keep the ball back in your stance. Make sure your hands are ahead of the ball, with the shaft angled towards the target. Let your weight favour your front foot, the left foot. This encourages a descending angle of attack into impact.

2 The backswing is a simple movement whereby the triangular relationship established at address between your arms and your shoulders is maintained as the club moves away from the ball. The weight distribution remains the same, still favouring the left side. The trouble for the majority of golfers starts when the backswing is either too short or too long for the shot in question.

3 As your arms and body begin the transition from backward to forward motion, a softness in your hands and wrists produces a slight lag in your wrists and a sense that your hands are leading the clubhead down towards the ball. It is a subtle move, but a decisive one, especially on a shot as short as this. It is an essential ingredient of a crisply struck chip shot.

4 Through the hitting zone, the contact should be ball-then-turf, the hallmark of all good players, and a skill that allows good control of spin and trajectory. Through impact, make sure your hands stay ahead of the clubhead as your body turns through. This coordination is extremely important – if your body stops moving, the club tends to overtake your hands and it is easy to strike the ball poorly as a result.

5 Keep your eyes down until the ball is well on its way. Note the economy of movement; almost perfect symmetry either side of the ball. It is such a tidy action with no wasted motion. With shots such as this there should always be a sense of natural acceleration through the ball.

Organize your set-up to make chips seem easy

If you have a fundamental problem striking your chips cleanly, then the prospect of playing any shot from around the green can be intimidating. In this case, it is likely that your set-up is to blame. Even those who consider themselves reasonable chippers would be wise to take this opportunity to revisit the basics. This simple exercise – which can be done at home, in the garden, or at the course – will ensure that you have the correct address position.

Left arm
The shaft of the club and your left arm form a straight line

Hands
Position your hands only slightly further forward than the clubhead

Weight
Sixty per cent of the weight is on the left foot

1 Stand with your feet, hips, and shoulders slightly open to the target (if you imagine the target as 12 o'clock, align yourself to 11 o'clock). Your feet should be only 15–20cm (6–8in) apart.

2 Place the ball back in your stance: opposite the right instep. Settle your weight to favour the leading foot. A ratio of 40 per cent of your weight on your right foot and 60 per cent on your left is ideal for a chip shot.

3 Place the clubhead behind the ball and move your hands forward so that your left arm and the shaft of the club form a straight line down to the ball. The clubface should be positioned so that it is aiming straight at the target.

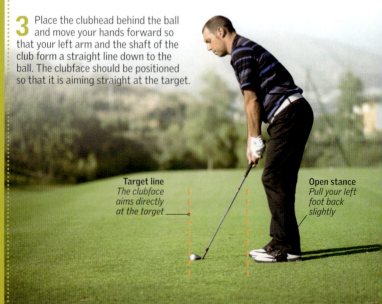

Target line
The clubface aims directly at the target

Open stance
Pull your left foot back slightly

Go back low, then release and hold

The technique described here applies to a medium-length chip of about 12m (13yd). However, for shots of various lengths, you can still apply the same techniques described in this drill – the only thing that changes is the length of your backswing (shorter to send the ball a lesser distance; longer to send it a greater distance).

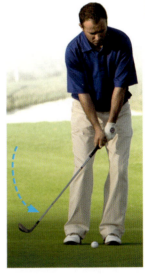

1 Assume the address position as in Drill 1 (see opposite). In your sweep, keep the clubhead low to the ground for the first 30cm (12in). Stop your backswing when your hands reach 8 o'clock.

2 Moving to the downswing, you should feel a softness in your hands ("lag"). This prevents the clubhead overtaking your hands before impact.

3 When you are familiar with these movements, you can then move on to hitting a ball.

COACHING TIP

Your body must move, even in a swing that is as short as this. As your arms swing back and forth, your body rotates backwards and through, everything works in harmony. If your body is motionless in your downswing, the clubhead will pass your hands before impact, and the club will meet the ball on an upward path, which is not desirable.

Brush the grass to find the perfect ball position

It is amazing how many golfers put the ball too far forward in their stance for chip shots. Although having the ball forward in your stance may feel comfortable, it can also cause problems with ball-striking: either you hit the ball on the up or hit the turf before the ball – both scenarios are disastrous. However, this drill will confirm the ideal spot to place the ball in your stance.

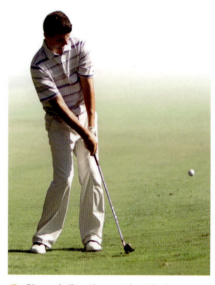

1 Stand on an area of closely mown grass. For the moment, do not position a ball. Make some swings, based on the techniques described in Drills 1 and 2 (see pp.92–93). Note where the clubhead first comes into contact with the ground. This is where you need to position the ball in your stance to ensure clean contact.

2 Place a ball on the spot described in step 1. Swing as before, but let the ball get in the way of the swinging club. You should strike the ball first and then the turf, leaving a small divot-mark if the ground is soft or the faintest bruising of the ground if conditions are hard underfoot.

" POSITIONING THE BALL FORWARD IN YOUR STANCE MAY CAUSE A POOR STROKE. "

COACHING TIP

Drill 1 (see p.92) explained that with a chip shot your impact position is virtually identical to your address position. Once you have found the ideal ball position, think in terms of recreating your address position at the moment of impact. This will promote the necessary ball-then-turf contact.

Play off a hard surface for a clean strike

This exercise highlights the benefits of practising from a tough spot to improve your overall technique. Although it is challenging at first, the drill ultimately improves your chipping action and makes playing normal chip shots seem simple. This will boost your level of confidence around the greens, which is a valuable asset to have.

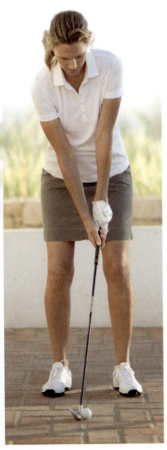

Hands
At impact your hands should be ahead of the ball

Impact
The clubface should first strike the ball, not the bare surface

1 Place a ball on a hard, bare surface, such as tarmac, or paving stones – anything that has no give in it. Use an old pitching wedge that you do not mind scratching. Put the ball back in your stance and push your hands forwards, and body-weight to your left side – refer to the keys to a good set-up outlined in Drill 1 (see p.92).

2 Hit some short chip shots of no more than 18m (20yd). For now, a target is irrelevant: the aim of this exercise is to strike the ball cleanly from an unforgiving surface. Keep your hands in front of the clubhead all the way into the hitting area. This will help prevent your clubhead hitting the bare surface before it reaches the ball. After a few tries, you should achieve some success. Next time you play a chip shot from grass, it will look far more inviting.

Create a downward strike for crisp chips

One of the worst crimes you can commit while chipping is to try to help the ball into the air with a scooping motion through impact. For short shots you need to hit down on the ball in order to make it go up. This drill shows the benefits of this technique.

1 Place a ball on a good lie, and position a headcover about 20cm (8in) behind it. At address, your hands must be ahead of the clubhead and the ball opposite your right instep.

2 Hit a chip shot of about 18m (20yd). To avoid hitting the headcover you have to strike down on the ball. This produces the ball-then-turf contact, a good ball-flight, and a bit of backspin on landing. If you try to scoop the ball into air, the clubhead will collide with the headcover during your downswing.

A BARE LEFT HAND CAN OFFER EXTRA TOUCH AND FEEL

As mentioned in the "Putting" section, most golfers putt with their bare hands. This gives a more delicate feel for the putter throughout the stroke. Many of the world's top golfers find this also applies to chip shots (the enhanced grip that a glove offers for long shots is not required for most short shots). You too might consider the benefits of chipping without a glove. However, you must find an "outer limit" (determined according to personal preference), after which you wear a glove. Stick to this limit so that you are never undecided about whether to play a chip with or without a glove. Chipping with bare hands might be a welcome change.

BARE HANDS
Many golfers take their glove off to chip, as this enhances control of the club.

Clip a tee-peg to promote a free swing

In a full swing, the clubhead travels so fast that there is no danger of the club stopping at impact. But with chipping, where the swing is short and delicacy is often required, it is easy to stub the clubhead into the ground behind the ball. The turf, instead of the ball, then soaks up the energy. This drill shows you how to be more positive in your approach to chipping, encouraging you to make a freer swing of the clubhead.

1 Tee up a ball about 1cm (³/₈in) off the ground. Address it as you would in case of a normal chip, using your pitching wedge.

2 Make a smooth, free swing of the club: focus on flattening the tee-peg into the ground at impact (below). This helps you to accelerate your clubhead through the hitting area. Try to ignore the ball. When you succeed in flattening the tee-peg, you will see yourself producing nicely flighted chips. Repeat the step a few times.

FLATTENED TEE-PEG

Try the "Bellied Wedge" shot from the collar of rough

One of the most perplexing dilemmas for golfers is when the ball rests against the collar of rough bordering the apron of the green. In this situation, neither a putter nor a wedge seems to be the appropriate club. The solution is a shot called the "Bellied Wedge" shot, which involves striking the equator of the ball with the leading edge of the clubhead.

Clubhead position
The leading edge should be level with the ball's equator

1 Using your pitching wedge, adopt your putting grip and posture (see pp.132–33). Choke down on the club, as this enhances your control of the stroke.

2 Hover the clubhead so that the leading edge is level with the ball's equator (see p.101). This way the club will not become snagged in the rough.

3 Keep your head and body still, and make a firm-wristed stroke back and forth. Ensure your wrists barely hinge – this is the "dead-hands" technique.

4 Strike the middle of the ball with the leading edge of the clubhead. The ball might slightly hop, but it should roll like a putt thereafter.

Try the "toe-poke" with a putter

You might have seen a few tour professionals striking the ball with the toe-end of the putter when playing a shot from the collar of rough around the green. This technique might seem unorthodox, but there is considerable logic to the shot, which is known as a "toe-poke". Although it is close to the flag, the collar of rough creates a very awkward lie. The tendency is to play too delicate a shot from this position, leaving the ball well short. The toe-poke is a useful remedy for this dangerous inclination.

1 Place a ball against the collar of rough beside the apron of a green. Now, instead of reaching for your wedge, take your putter out of your golf bag.

2 Hold the putter so that the toe-end of the club is hovering behind the ball's equator. The end of the club should also be pointing towards the hole.

3 Make a short, sharp, stabbing stroke and aim to strike the centre of the ball. You will find that there is no interference from the grass behind the ball – the primary reason for playing the shot in this way. The ball will pop into the air before the topspin takes effect, allowing it to roll on to the putting surface.

Play a mini-hook shot to give your chips more run

This advanced chip shot is best described as a miniature hook. Before you attempt it, keep in mind that a hook produces right-to-left spin, which makes the ball run further than normal. This makes it a useful shot to have in your repertoire when you have a lot of green between yourself and the pin. The drill given here helps you perfect the shot.

1 Select a short iron, such as an 8-iron. Position the ball well back in your stance, opposite your right toe, and place your hands well in front of the clubhead (even more so than for a normal chip shot). Also, feel that you align your body a little right of the target, with the clubface aiming straight at the flag.

Practise with a lofted wood

Chipping with a lofted wood has become popular since the likes of Tiger Woods and Greg Norman have played this shot in major competitions. This practice drill demonstrates how you can use the lofted wood effectively for shots close to the green.

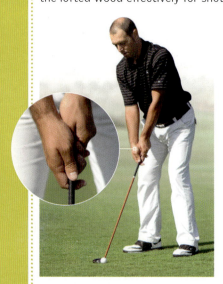

1 Take a 3- or 4-wood, and choke down on the grip so that your lower hand almost touches the metal of the shaft.

2 Adopt your normal chipping set-up. Stand a little taller and further from the ball than when using a wedge (or your hands and arms become tucked into midriff, leaving no room for movement).

2 Take the club back on a path that is distinctly more on the inside than for a regular chip shot.

3 Swing the club into impact on the same path, so that the clubhead travels right of the target. This in-to-out path imparts the right-to-left spin, making the ball fly low and roll more.

> " THE LOFTED WOOD CAN BE EFFECTIVELY USED FOR **SHOTS CLOSE TO THE GREEN**. "

3 Make a putting stroke (see pp.130–45), swinging the clubhead low to the ground with little wrist hinge. This makes the clubhead brush the ground, and the ball roll quickly over the green.

HOVER THE CLUB ON ROUGH CHIPS

Hovering the club at address promotes an unimpeded takeaway and enhances the quality of your strike. If the ball is lying in the rough, hover the blade of the club around the ball's equator. It makes the clubhead move away from the ball without getting caught in the grass on the way back, which can upset the rhythm of your swing.

This technique also lets you raise the base of your swing by just a fraction. This means that you are less likely to bury the clubhead in the grass behind the ball and should instead make a better strike.

RAISE YOUR GAME
Hovering the clubhead behind the ball in the rough promotes a smoother takeaway, as the clubhead does not get snagged.

Use upturned umbrellas

To be a good chipper, you have to control the height, carry, spin, and roll of the ball. The following exercise is based on a popular practice drill, but with an added twist to enhance your judgement of two of the four key elements: height and carry.

1 Stick two open umbrellas into the ground, approximately 5m (5¹/₂yd) apart. Place a batch of balls about 5m (5¹/₂yd) from one of the umbrellas.

2 Using your pitching wedge, alternate hitting one ball to the closer umbrella and the next ball to the further one. Try to land every ball in an umbrella.

Monitor your swing path

In a chip shot, the clubhead travels through impact at a slower speed than with a full iron shot, which makes it hard to monitor the path of the clubhead. The following drill can show you how to do this.

Keep your hands and weight forward

1 Place a club about one clubface-length on the other side of the ball, parallel to the ball-to-target line. Address the ball with a pitching wedge. Keep the ball back in your stance (see Drill 1, p.92).

2 Play a chip shot. Your club should travel on an inside arc during the backswing, parallel to the obstruction through the hitting zone, before arcing to the inside in the followthrough.

Throw some balls

This drill is designed to train you to visualize shots before playing them. It uses the simple action of throwing a ball to improve your understanding of height and roll. A better grasp of these key concepts will be of great benefit to your chipping.

1 Stand about 27m (30yd) from a flag. Have to hand at least 10 balls and a selection of clubs, from a 7-iron to a sand wedge. Lob a ball underarm, and try to finish as close as possible to the flag. Use a low trajectory, which will produce plenty of roll. After a couple of tries you should find your range quite accurately.

2 Now throw a ball underarm high into the air so that it bounces near the flag and does not roll far. You will find it much more difficult to get the balls to finish close to the flag. Not only that, but also the general dispersion of the "high" balls will probably be more erratic. Keep throwing balls, always varying the height and roll.

3 Now hit some chip shots. Think of the trajectory and roll you achieved with your throws, and try to recreate these by selecting clubs with different lofts. Again you will find that the low shots nearly always finish closer than those hit high.

Rehearse, look, and hit

Many golfers chip poorly because they fail to make use of their natural "touch" and hand-eye co-ordination. By practising chipping as outlined in the following drill, you will use these attributes to improve your performance around the greens.

1 Set yourself up 10m (11yd) from the flag. Make practice swings, but look at the target not the ground. Think about the force and length needed for the shot.

2 Address the ball, take one look at the hole, and hit the chip. Do not hesitate, just recreate the same swing that you practised in step 1.

Rock the shaft

The relationship between your upper body and your arms is critical for any golf shot, even chip shots. These two core elements of your swing must work together to ensure reliable and consistent shots. This drill trains your body and arms to work together.

1 Trap a club under your armpits so that the shaft is horizontal across your chest. Take a 9-iron and assume the normal address position, while keeping the horizontal shaft in place.

2 Rock the shaft by turning your body back and through. Let your arms respond to this movement, and you will find the club track a neat path. Ensure that the shaft stays against your chest.

Add and subtract hours

Most golfers make too long a backswing and then decelerate into impact. This drill is based on the principle of determining your swing length using positions on an imaginary clockface. It will also help you learn to accelerate into the ball on every chip shot.

7 o'clock

Followthrough
The club swings through further than it went back

4 o'clock

BACKSWING

1 Make a backswing with a pitching wedge where your hands swing to 7 o'clock. Then, accelerate through the hitting zone, and swing your hands to 4 o'clock, so that the followthrough is longer than your backswing. Note how far the ball travels.

8 o'clock

Followthrough
Again accelerate the club through further than you swung it back

3 o'clock

BACKSWING

2 Let your hands swing to 8 o'clock. Then, take an hour off the followthrough so that your hands are at 3 o'clock. Your followthrough will be longer than your backswing, making the ball travel further.

Use a weak grip to keep the face open

Some of the world's greatest chippers play short, delicate chip shots with a weak left-hand grip. This technique helps keep the clubface open through the hitting zone, which promotes a higher- and softer-landing ball flight, enabling the most delicate of chips. Using a weak left-hand grip is a technique that is well worth practising – give this routine a try next time you are working on your chipping.

1 Place about 12 balls on a good lie on the fairway. Play a standard chip shot with a pitching wedge, using your regular chipping technique. Observe the way the ball travels through the air and the amount of roll there is after landing.

2 Now weaken your grip by rotating your left hand, so that you can barely see the second knuckle on the back of your left hand.

3 Hit another chip shot. Since your weak grip effectively keeps the clubface more open through impact, this should translate into a slightly higher, floated trajectory with much less run on landing. Alternate between hitting chip shots with your regular grip and others with a weak grip.

Try chipping using your putting technique

Any idea that might make the short game easier is well worth considering. The technique described in the following drill is employed by some of the world's best players, which is reason enough to give it a try. It can be applied to a wide variety of clubs, from a pitching wedge down to an 8-iron, depending on the circumstances.

1 Adopt your putting grip (see Drill 1, p.132) instead of your regular full-swing grip.

> " CHIPPING USING YOUR PUTTING TECHNIQUE HELPS **IMPROVE YOUR CHIPS**. "

Grip
Choke down on the club's grip for extra control

Takeaway
Sweep the clubhead away with your hands and arms

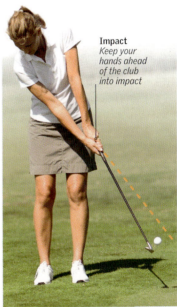

Impact
Keep your hands ahead of the club into impact

2 Nudge your hands ahead of the clubhead and ball at address. The shaft of the club should now be leaning noticeably towards the target.

3 Now simply replicate the swing action you would use for a long putt. As you swing your arms back and through impact, it is important that your hands remain ahead of the clubhead.

Bunker play

For most club golfers, bunker play creates more fear and problems than any other type of shot. This cannot be attributed to the degree of difficulty involved because, ironically, the standard bunker shot is one of the most forgiving strokes in golf. For one thing, you do not even have to hit the ball. With a sound technique you can hit the sand between 2.5cm (1in) and 6cm (2½in) behind the ball and produce an acceptable result.

As you work your way through this section, your fear of bunker play will evaporate. You will learn that long-range bunker shots are no harder than normal iron shots, and from short range you will start to finish the hole in two strokes. This section of the book will improve your sand performance, while the sequence below will show you how to make the perfect bunker shot – as demonstrated by Freddie Jacobsen.

1 Adopt perfect alignment for a greenside bunker shot; your feet, hips, and shoulders should be aligned slightly to the left of the flag, with the clubface aiming to the right of that. This stance promotes the desired out-to-in swing path, while the open clubface helps the wide flange on the sole of the sand-wedge to slide through the sand. These elements combine to produce a straight shot.

2 Now let your hands and arms swing the club upwards, while your body continues to turn. This is an essential combination, even on short shots.

3 Make sure that your clubface is still wide open – crucial for good greenside bunker play. The club-shaft should point to the left of the flag, across the line, making it easy to swing the club down on the correct path and plane for optimum contact in the sand.

4 Swing the clubhead freely through the sand under the ball. This step again highlights the importance of the correct address position. The open stance facilitates the out-to-in swing path, while the open clubface ensures that the clubhead slides through the sand and "splashes" the ball out of the bunker and towards the flag.

5 Despite the feel inherent in this type of shot – the ball floats upwards and forwards on a "soft" trajectory – the positive swing should be evident in the length of your followthrough. It is an aggressive yet controlled motion.

Open your feet, hips, shoulders, and the clubface

In golf there is nothing more futile than trying to hit good shots from a poor address position, and this is never more so than when you are playing from sand. Next time you practise your bunker play, use the following drill to rehearse and become familiar with the perfect set-up for a greenside bunker shot.

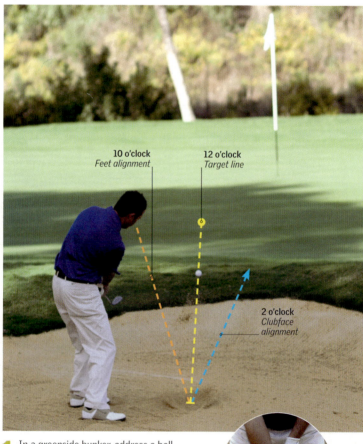

10 o'clock
Feet alignment

12 o'clock
Target line

2 o'clock
Clubface alignment

1 In a greenside bunker, address a ball as you would in an iron shot. Loosen your left-hand grip. Hold the bottom of the club's grip with your right hand, and turn the club clockwise. Imagine the flag at 12 o'clock, and turn until the clubface aims at 2 o'clock. Reapply your left hand, and place your right hand on the grip.

2 Move into an open stance, so that the alignment of your feet, hips, and shoulders aims at 10 o'clock (to the left of the flag). Make sure that the clubface remains open, aiming right of the target.

3 Shuffle your feet down into the sand. This not only gives you a secure footing on an insecure surface, but also gives you a feel for the sand's texture.

Make right-handed swings
to feel the splash

One of the most important things to understand about bunker play is that the bounce on your sand wedge is designed to help you but can only do so if your technique is correct. The following drill helps you appreciate how the sand wedge moves through the sand and introduces some freedom into your technique.

1 Step into a bunker with your sand wedge. For now, do not worry about a ball.

2 Assume a good address position (see Drill 1, opposite), but hold the club with your right hand only.

3 Make one-handed swings, and almost "throw" the clubhead into the sand. Allow your right arm to straighten, and your wrist to unhinge. Try to make the clubhead slide through the sand. You should be left with a shallow cut of sand, about 30cm (12in) long.

Draw a line in the sand to guide your path

It is now time to hit some proper greenside bunker shots. This practice drill involves drawing a line in the sand to indicate the ideal swing path through impact. Remember that you cannot do this during a round of golf because touching the sand with your club before playing the shot is against the rules.

1 Place a ball in the sand and address it (see Drill 1, p.110). Use the butt-end of the club to draw a line in the sand along the line of your toes. Then draw another line that extends about 20cm (8in) either side of the ball, parallel to the first line.

2 Swing the clubhead back along the second line, hinging your wrists a little earlier than you would while hitting a chip shot. This will set the club on a slightly more upright swing plane. Do not forget to turn your body as you swing the club upwards.

3 Splash the clubhead into the sand behind the ball (see Drill 4, opposite), again swinging the clubhead along the line in the sand through impact. This implies that in essence you are swinging the club along the line of your toes, to the left of the target, with the clubface slightly open. This exercise will help you propel the ball out of the sand and towards the flag.

Draw a line in the sand to focus on your strike

Just like Drill 3 (see opposite), this drill involves drawing a line in the sand. But rather than assisting your alignment and swing path, it helps in the development of another important element of bunker play: learning to consistently hit the right spot in the sand behind the ball.

1 Use the butt-end of your sand wedge to draw one long line in the sand, perpendicular to the ball-to-target line.

2 Place a row of balls 5cm (2in) in front of that line. Make sure that there is at least a 25-cm (10-in) gap between each ball.

" AIM TO **SWING THE CLUBHEAD** DOWN ON THE LINE AND **FREELY** THROUGH THE SAND. **"**

3 Play each ball along the line in turn. As always, make sure that your stance and the clubface are open. Swing the clubhead down on the line in the sand, and accelerate through the sand under the ball. You do not have to worry about the ball because if your technique is good, it will splash out every time.

Throw a stone to recreate the right-hand action

Drill 3 (see p.112) explained that you should not release the club when playing a bunker shot so as to ensure that the clubface stays open through impact. Here is a practice drill that will help you become accustomed to how your right hand should work when playing a bunker shot. It involves a movement apparently unrelated to golf yet which comes naturally to almost everyone.

1 Take a stone, and throw it as if trying to skim it across a body of water. Notice that on drawing your throwing arm backwards, your right shoulder turns down and under your chin as your body opens up, and your right hand swings through to throw the stone on a flat trajectory. Repeat this action to monitor your right-hand moves and body-turns.

Try to imagine your right hand moving as it did to throw the stone

2 Step into a bunker with your sand wedge, and make a practice swing. Try to imagine your right hand moving as it did to throw the stone. In your downswing, your right shoulder should again turn down as your body opens up, and your right hand should swing flat so that the clubhead slides through the sand on a shallow trajectory.

3 Now hit some shots, recreating the sensations experienced in step 2. Let the clubhead splash freely through the sand under the ball.

Focus on the sand, not the ball

Walter Hagen, a flamboyant figure in the first half of the 20th century (and one of the greatest golfers of all time), said that bunker shots should be the easiest shots in the game because you do not even have to hit the ball. This thought can make playing a good bunker shot more straightforward, as this drill will illustrate.

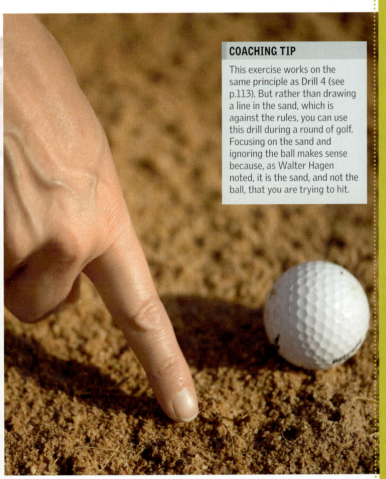

COACHING TIP

This exercise works on the same principle as Drill 4 (see p.113). But rather than drawing a line in the sand, which is against the rules, you can use this drill during a round of golf. Focusing on the sand and ignoring the ball makes sense because, as Walter Hagen noted, it is the sand, and not the ball, that you are trying to hit.

1 Step into the sand and set up for a regular greenside bunker shot from a good lie.

2 Instead of looking at the ball, which is what you do on every shot, focus on a spot in the sand 5cm (2in) behind the ball (above). Although this might seem a little strange at first, resist the temptation to look at the ball.

3 Keep focusing on the sand as you swing. If you make a good swing, and accelerate the clubhead into the right spot in the sand, the ball will naturally fly out of the bunker every time. Hit several balls using this technique.

Double your swing-length from grass to sand

Golf is not an exact science. The way to approach a shot cannot usually be determined using special formulas. However, the following drill will show you a simple equation that will help you judge the distance of your greenside bunker shots.

> " YOUR ACCELERATION RATE THROUGH IMPACT SHOULD **REMAIN THE SAME** FOR BOTH THE SHOTS. "

1 Find a greenside bunker that is approximately 10m (11yd) from the flag. Play a chip shot with your sand wedge from beside the bunker. Select a good lie, and try to leave the ball as close as possible to the flag.

2 Now step into the bunker, and double the length of the swing that you just made from grass. Try to feel that your rate of acceleration through impact, and the overall tempo of your swing, is the same as for the previous shot. The cushioning effect of the sand trapped between the clubface and the ball should ensure that the ball travels the same distance as the chip.

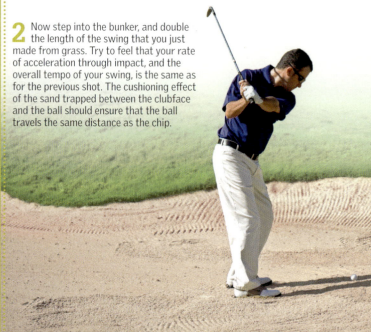

Try out two methods of varying your distance

Opinion is divided when it comes to recommending the ideal way to vary the distance you hit a bunker shot. Most golf instructors say it is best to take the same amount of sand every time and vary the swing-length to generate different distances. But a few say you should instead vary the amount of sand you take at impact.

CLOSE TO THE BALL
Hit 1cm (³⁄₈in) behind the ball, and see how far it flies.

FURTHER BEHIND THE BALL
Hit 8cm (3¹⁄₄in) behind the ball, and see how far it flies.

1 Push three tee-pegs at random into any green with a bunker. Select your sand wedge and step into the bunker.

2 Separate six balls into batches of three. Hit one ball to each of the three tee-pegs using the method whereby you take the same amount of sand every time. Start with the closest tee-peg, and make progressively longer swings to send the other two balls further each time. Now, hit the remaining balls using the technique whereby you take maximum amount of sand to send the first ball to the nearest tee-peg.

Match your backswing and followthrough

When playing a greenside bunker shot, you must accelerate the clubhead through impact to ensure that there is sufficient energy to create a wave of sand big enough to propel the ball from the bunker. This drill will help you accelerate the club through the sand every time.

Backswing
Note the position your hands reach in the backswing

Followthrough
Swing the club so that your followthrough is longer than your backswing

1 Find a greenside bunker about 18m (20yd) from the flag. Rehearse a backswing, and note how far back your hands and arms go. There is no need for a ball at this stage.

2 Splash the clubhead into the sand, accelerating it so that it goes further through than you went back. Place a ball on a good lie in the sand, then hit a shot, focusing on making your followthrough longer than the backswing.

ALWAYS COVER YOUR TRACKS

Once you have finished playing a bunker shot, use the rake provided to smooth over your footprints and the trough left by the clubhead splashing through the sand. Try to leave the bunker in a state in which you would wish to find it. This is simple etiquette (see pp.20–21) that ensures that every golfer has an equal chance of ending up with a good lie in the sand. You deserve this; and so too does the golfer playing in the group behind you. This advice is meant for amateur players as well as well-experienced golfers.

RAKE THE SAND
It is part of the etiquette of golf to leave a bunker just as you would hope to find it. There is nothing more disheartening than finding your ball has come to rest in the middle of a deep footprint.

Build a cleaner strike for long-range bunker shots

The following practice drill is designed to improve your long-range bunker shots. The exercise will teach you how to strike the ball cleanly, with no interference from sand between the clubface and the ball, which – unlike in the case of greenside bunker shots – is exactly what you should do in fairway bunkers. The benefits gained from this drill are just as great for your general iron play, too.

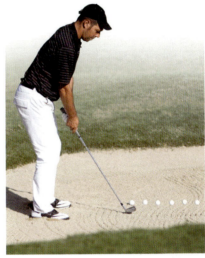

1 Find a fairway bunker without a major front lip, and with enough space to hit shots from a flat lie. Draw a narrow line in the sand, and place as many balls as possible along the line.

2 With your 7-iron, address the first ball. Use the same set-up you would use for an iron shot (see pp.24–27). Shuffle your feet into the sand for a secure footing. As this lowers the base of your swing, choke down on the grip by about 2.5cm (1in) to compensate.

3 Now hit shots with a full swing; the object here is to strike the ball cleanly. For this, you need to strike the ball first, then the sand, which requires a descending blow. If you are playing correctly, there will be a small mark in the sand after the spot where the ball was. Do not scoop the ball out of the sand.

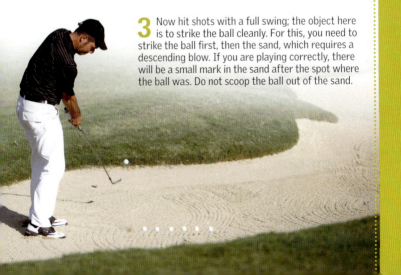

The intermediate bunker shot

This drill answers one of the most commonly asked questions about bunker play: should you strike intermediate-length bunker shots – those in the 40–50m (44–55yd) range – cleanly or with a bit of sand at impact? The following exercise will eliminate all confusion.

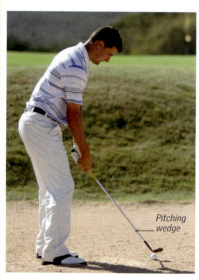

Pitching wedge

1 Imagine a flag 40–50m (44–55yd) from the bunker at 12 o'clock (see p.110). Align feet, hips, and shoulders to 11 o'clock (left of the flag). Open the clubface so that it aims between 12 and 1 o'clock (right of the flag).

2 Take less sand than you would from a greenside bunker – aim to strike the sand 1cm (³/₈in) behind the ball. This is, however, different for greenside and fairway bunker shots.

3 Imagine your head at 12 o'clock and the ball at 6 o'clock (see p.81). Swing your hands back to 10 o'clock and aim to strike the sand in the spot identified in step 2. Your open stance produces an out-to-in swing path (see pp.30–31), which combined with an open clubface, produces a shot with a touch of sidespin.

Be bolder on an upslope

There will be occasions where your ball will cling to a slope, especially on courses that use soft, powdery sand. At these times, your normal bunker technique will not suffice: you have to be creative with your set-up, and adapt your swing in order to counteract the effects of the slope. This drill will show you how to do this.

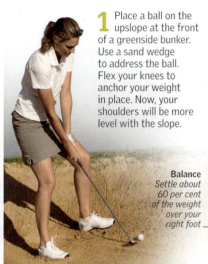

1 Place a ball on the upslope at the front of a greenside bunker. Use a sand wedge to address the ball. Flex your knees to anchor your weight in place. Now, your shoulders will be more level with the slope.

Balance
Settle about 60 per cent of the weight over your right foot

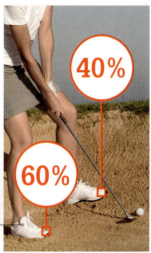

40%

60%

CORRECT WEIGHT DISTRIBUTION

40%

60%

2 In your backswing, keep your knees flexed and your head steady. Do not sway backwards or forwards, as this will upset your balance, making it difficult to strike the correct spot in the sand.

3 As you change direction from backswing to downswing, keep your weight on your right foot, and focus on swinging the club up the slope through impact.

Chase the ball

The previous drill (see p.121) covered one of the simple sloping-lie shots. This drill covers a more difficult option – when the ball comes to rest on a downslope. Do not ignore practising these shots, however difficult they might seem.

Steep strike
Swing your club back in a steep arc

40%

60%

1 Take your sand wedge and place a ball on a downslope. Distribute most of your weight on to your lower left foot and introduce knee flex. Your shoulders should be almost level with the slope.

2 Hinge your wrists early to send the club upwards on a steep arc. This enables you to strike down steeply into the sand behind the ball. Keep your weight steady.

3 Keep your hands ahead of the clubhead, and hit down into the sand behind the ball. Feel as if the clubhead is chasing the ball down the slope so that it stays low to the surface into the followthrough.

HIT FROM THE HIGH FOOT

Here is a rule of thumb that simplifies playing from sloping lies in the sand: always play the ball towards your higher foot. On a downslope, the clubhead comes into contact with the sand earlier in the downswing, which means that you need the ball back in your stance to obtain the correct contact. On an upslope, the clubhead meets the sand later in its downswing arc, so you need the ball further forward in your stance for a good strike.

SIMPLIFY SLOPING LIES
Remember to address the ball towards your high foot: your right on a downslope; your left on an upslope (as shown).

Play the ball above your feet

In addition to the slopes dealt with in Drills 12 and 13 (see pp.121–22), you may also encounter sideslope lies in bunkers. These shots are just as intimidating to the uninformed but equally manageable if you adapt your stance and swing to suit the slope. This drill will examine the situation in which the ball comes to rest well above the level of your feet.

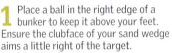

Stance

Target line

1 Place a ball in the right edge of a bunker to keep it above your feet. Ensure the clubface of your sand wedge aims a little right of the target.

2 Grip so that your right hand almost touches the metal. Make a rounded backswing, taking an inside path that is more behind you than upwards.

3 Swing down on the same path you went back on, moving the clubhead from inside the target line to right of the line through impact. As with greenside bunker play, identify a spot behind the ball, and splash the clubhead down into the sand at that point.

Steady yourself when the ball is below your feet

Arguably the toughest bunker shot is when the ball is below your feet – if the ball is close to the edge of the bunker, you will not even be able to stand in the sand. You may have to play the shot on your knees. Even assuming you can stand in the sand, it is still difficult to maintain your balance.

Sand wedge

1 Place a ball in the left edge of a bunker, so that it sits below the level of your feet. As you have to reach down to the ball, hold the club so that your left hand is at the top of the grip. Spread your feet further apart, as this lowers your upper body, and you are closer to the ball. Bend over more from your waist, if necessary.

2 Open your stance so that it is aligned even further left than for a regular greenside bunker shot. This allows for the fact that the ball will fly right of where you aim when it is below your feet.

3 Swing your hands and arms back, and use your wrists to hinge the club steeply upwards. Keep your head at the same level throughout, as this will help you maintain your height as you swing the clubhead down into the sand.

Open wide for a very short splash

Although long-range and intermediate-length bunker shots are tricky, the toughest sand shots of all are those where you need to carry the ball only 3–5m (3–5yd). This drill shows you a more effective technique than taking a normal-length backswing and decelerating into impact to stop the ball flying too far.

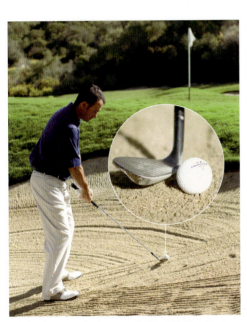

1 Open your stance so much that your chest virtually faces the target, and spread your feet 30cm (12in) further apart than you would for a normal greenside bunker shot. This set-up will probably feel odd, but it is necessary.

2 Open the clubface to a greater degree than for any other shot. In fact, the clubface should be so open that you could almost rest a glass of water on it. Swing the club back along your body line. Your backswing will be way outside the normal swing path but totally appropriate for this type of shot.

3 Accelerate the clubhead down on the same path as your backswing, so that the clubhead travels on a severe out-to-in path (see pp.30–31). This swing path, combined with the massively open clubface, means that the club will slice through the sand, and the ball should rise sharply, with a more upward than forward momentum.

Practise in preparation for the worst

The drills in this section have covered the skills required to make you a better bunker player. Now for the ultimate practice drill – one that enables you to apply your imagination and technique to a variety of different shots.

1 Place 10 balls in a bunker. Position the first ball at the left edge of the bunker, below your feet level; and the tenth ball at the right edge of the bunker, above your feet level. Give the other balls a different lie.

2 Work your way along the line, playing each ball in turn. The sand wedge is best for most shots, but have other clubs, such as a pitching wedge and a 9-iron, if you wish to experiment as you go along.

3 Size up each lie, visualize how the ball will come out of the sand, and try to match your technique and club selection to suit the shot.

MATCH BOUNCE TO THE TEXTURE OF SAND

You can buy sand wedges with a variety of degrees of bounce. Your requirements will depend on the type of sand used on the course at which you play most often. The softer the sand, the more bounce you need on the sole of the sand wedge; on heavier sand you need less bounce. Equipment requirements are looked at in greater detail in The Basics section (see pp.14–17), but this is a point worth making before leaving the bunker and moving on to the putting green.

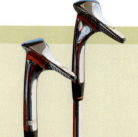

BOUNCE ON SAND WEDGE
Less bounce (left) suits heavier sand; more bounce (right) is best for soft sand.

Experiment with different clubs from sand

The sand wedge is designed to make bunker play as easy as possible. But it is not the only club you can use from sand. With some skill and know-how, using other clubs can increase your options and flexibility in the bunker. This drill will enhance your repertoire of shots.

1 Step into a greenside bunker with a sand wedge, a pitching wedge, a 9-iron, and about 12 balls. With your sand wedge, hit two normal greenside bunker shots. Observe the way the ball flies and how far it runs.

2 Now switch to your pitching wedge. Open the clubface, so that it slides through the sand, and commit to making a positive swing to stop the clubhead becoming buried. The ball will fly on a lower trajectory.

3 Finally, take your 9-iron. Open your stance and the clubface again. You will find that the same swing produces an even flatter trajectory with even more run on landing.

" A **9-IRON OR PITCHING WEDGE** IS USEFUL FOR PLAYING A **RUNNING BUNKER SHOT** ACROSS A LONG GREEN. **"**

On the Green

Putting

Although the putting stroke is very short in comparison to the full swing, it is open to greater personal interpretation than any other shot. One characteristic that all great putters share is a consistent stroke where all the moving parts complement one another perfectly. With this type of stroke, the ball will travel along the chosen line at the required speed relative to the length of the putt.

As putting accounts for about 40 per cent of the total shots played in a round, it would be a terrible mistake to neglect this department of the game. The following section will give you a thorough understanding of the mechanics of putting, which will enable you to incorporate the essential ingredients of an effective stroke into your personal style. The sequence below will show you how to make the perfect putt – as demonstrated by Robert Karlsson.

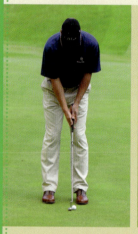  

1 First and foremost, your grip should be neutral, with your palms facing one another in the form of a comfortable and correct grip. Position your eyes directly over the ball.

2 Make sure your shoulders, arms, hands and the putter all move away together to produce a smooth and nicely synchronized start to the takeaway. The putter-head should stay very low to the ground. A useful method of keeping the lower half of the body stable is to keep the knees very still.

3 When you make the transition from backswing to downswing, there should be a softness in your wrists that causes the putter to momentarily lag behind your hands. This ensures that the putter does not overtake your hands at impact, which would cause the face to close and the ball to go left.

4 In putting, the impact position should be identical to the set-up. Let the putter travel just beyond the bottom of its swing arc at the moment of impact, which produces a slight upward strike that helps impart a good roll on the ball. Keep your head steady, ensuring that no unwanted upper body movement can upset the perfect path of the putter into and through impact.

5 Let your putter-head finish higher in the followthrough than it ever reached in the backswing, which is a product of smooth acceleration and an upward strike.

Form your putting grip

While there are three main types of recommended grip for the full swing (see pp.22–23), with putting there is much more choice. That said, however, conventional wisdom suggests that using the grip known as the "reverse overlap" is the best way to control the putter as you swing. Use this drill to form the reverse overlap.

1 Place your hands either side of the club's grip, with your palms facing each other, and each hand square to the target.

2 Place your left hand on the club, with your thumb pointing straight down the middle of the grip; keep your forefinger off the grip for now.

3 Place your right hand on the club, again with the thumb pointing down the grip. Wrap your right-hand fingers around the grip, and put your left forefinger over them. This is the reverse overlap. (Note: with the left forefinger, you can either extend it directly down the grip, above, or tuck it behind, step 4.)

4 Extend the forefinger of your right hand down the side of the grip, as this enhances your control of the putter. Exactly how far this finger reaches down the grip is again determined by personal preference. Hold the club at least as softly as in the full swing. Putting relies on delicate touch.

Take your putting posture

Good posture is important for a full swing. But it is critical to the success of your putting stroke, too. Ideally, you should adopt a posture at address that allows your arms to hang down – not totally straight, but tension-free for a smooth action back and forth. This simple routine will help you establish a good putting posture.

1 Stand up straight with the putter against your left leg. Flex your knees slightly and bend from your hips so that your arms hang limp from your shoulders. Jiggle your hands to relax your arms. Form your putting grip in the normal way (see Drill 1, opposite).

2 Note the key elements of this posture. Your arms should be slightly bent, with the elbows pointing in towards the ribcage. Think of your arms and shoulders as a triangle, and you will be producing the correct stroke. Your weight should be evenly balanced between both feet.

THE GEOMETRY OF A GOOD PUTT

From a worm's eye view, the putting stroke is saucer-shaped. The putterhead sweeps away from the ball on a gentle upward curve and comes down in the same way. At the bottom of its arc, it travels horizontally before following an upward curve through impact. For a good putting stroke, ensure that ball-contact occurs just after the putter reaches the bottom of its arc. This helps give the ball a smooth roll.

PERFECT SWING
In all the best putting strokes, the putter swings freely back and forth, with the ball merely getting in its way.

Check your ball position

Putting allows you more individuality than any other aspect of the game. But, whatever method you decide to employ, ensure that your eyes are directly over the ball in your address position. The following exercise enables you to fulfil this key requirement.

1 Assume your putting posture (see Drill 2, p.133), but do not place a ball on the ground. Take your right hand off the club, and hold a golf ball against the top of your nose, between your eyes.

2 Let the ball drop (you might have to move the club slightly). Take careful note of where the ball first strikes the ground. This spot is where you should position the ball in your putting stance.

Putterface alignment

Drill 5 (see opposite) touches on aiming the putter correctly, which is not easy. Tests have revealed that from a distance of 3m (3¹/₂yd), over half of professionals fail to aim the putterface within a 2.5cm (1in) margin either side of the hole. This drill will ensure that you are always aiming at the target.

1 Crouch down 3–4m (3¹/₂–4¹/₂yd) away from the hole on a green. Line up the face of your putter so that it is square with the hole.

2 Take your address position, without twisting the putter. Look back and forth from the putter to the hole. Try to memorize the position of your putter in relation to the hole. Hit a putt. The ball should travel straight to the hole.

Find the correct alignment

In a professional tournament, those at the top of the leaderboard seem to sink every putt within 2m (2yd) of the hole. Similarly at club level, in your best rounds, you are likely to hole your putts like a professional. This drill focuses your attention on the three key elements of successful short-range putting: putterface alignment at address, swing path, and putterface alignment at impact.

1 Find a straight putt on the green no more than 2m (2yd) from the hole. Place two clubs on the green on a straight path to the hole, with about 2.5cm (1in) to spare either side of the heel and toe of the putterhead. These two clubs will give you a visual reference to help you aim the putterface squarely at the hole and will also allow you to monitor the putter's swing path.

2 Place a ball directly between the two clubs, and take up your normal address position. If the putterface is at 90 degrees to the two parallel clubs, as it should be, you will be aiming straight at the hole. Make sure that the putter tracks a neat path between the rails in your backswing.

3 Swing the putter into the back of the ball. If the putterface is square at impact, the ball will roll into the hole. Maintain the triangle formed by your arms and shoulders at address, and adopt a soft grip pressure. Feel some "lag" – softness in the wrists – as you change direction from backswing to downswing.

Match your backswing to the distance

When you watch good putters in action, it is almost as if there is no "hit" as such; instead, the ball simply gets in the way of the swinging putterhead. This is a useful way to think of a putt, but you can only achieve this if your backswing-length matches the length of putt. This drill will help you learn this important golf skill.

1 Stand about 6m (6½yd) away from a hole, drop three balls, and address the first. Make a short backswing: no more than 10cm (4in) from the ball. To hole the ball from this position, you will have to jab the putter into the ball with an abrupt movement.

Keep your eyes down

The old adage, "keep your head down", has caused more faults in golfers' full swings than any other piece of advice because it prevents a good body pivot and free arm-swing through impact. But with putting, keeping your head down is an excellent idea. It ensures that your body is steady, which keeps the putter on a true path back and forth; this in turn promotes a controlled strike.

1 Place a coin under a ball, and adopt your address position. Make a backswing of comfortable length (the length of putt you hit is not important), keeping your eyes firmly fixed on the top of the ball.

2 As you strike the ball, focus on the coin. Doing so will ensure that your head remains still until the ball has started its journey towards the hole.

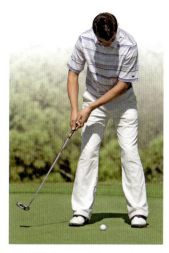

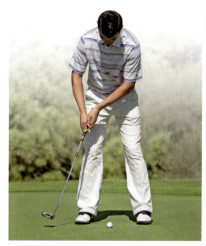

2 With the second ball, make an exaggerated backswing of approximately 50cm (20in). To hit the ball the correct distance, you will have to slow down in the hitting area.

3 Now, split the difference between the two backswing lengths in steps 2 and 3. You should now be able to accelerate the putter through the hitting area. This should feel like a swing, rather than a hit.

Check your aim and stroke

DRILL 08

The following drill will reveal two key pieces of information about your putting stroke: whether the putterface is aimed correctly, and if the path of your stroke is on the correct line. Many leading tour professionals have been known to rehearse this exercise – Nick Faldo even credited it as one of the secrets behind his 1992 Open Championship victory.

1 Locate a green, and set up a straight putt about 1m (1yd) from the hole. Address the ball, with the putterface sitting behind the ball, square to the hole.

2 Now brush the ball towards the hole with a smooth forward motion. Do not make a backswing. If the ball travels into the middle of the hole, you know the putt was successful.

Avoid excess wrist action

The conventional putting method involves a stroke controlled by the shoulders and arms, with a small amount of wrist action – referred to as "lag" (see p.135). This wrist movement promotes good rhythm and a smooth acceleration of the putter through the hitting zone. Excessive wrist action can upset the alignment of the putterface and disrupt your ability to control the distance of your putts.

1 Address a ball as normal, and trap another ball between your right wrist and the top of the grip on your putter.

Trap a ball
Make sure that the ball remains in place throughout the stroke

2 Hit some putts of about 8m (8¹/₂yd), making sure that the ball remains in place throughout the stroke. This prevents excessive wrist movement, which promotes a smooth, on-line stroke. If the ball falls to the ground, there is too much wrist action in your putting stroke.

COACHING TIP

Although there have been wonderful "wristy" putters in golfing history, such as multiple major winners Gary Player and Arnold Palmer, for most people this method is much less reliable than the more conventional technique advocated throughout this section. A wristy action is more difficult to repeat and increases the likelihood of inconsistent strikes and poor judgement of pace.

Make your stroke flow

Here is one of the best ways to promote a free swing of the putter in your stroke: a prerequisite for good judgement of distance. Although this exercise relates to one of the fundamental putting issues, because it requires you to putt with one hand only, a reasonable level of skill is needed.

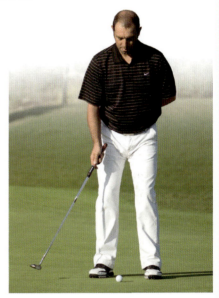

1 Grip the putter with your right hand, and keep your left hand in the pocket, or let it hang down.

2 Keep your grip pressure light, make a free swing, and let your wrist hinge slightly in response to the momentum of the putter changing direction from backswing to followthrough. This softness in your wrist encourages the putter to flow back and forth.

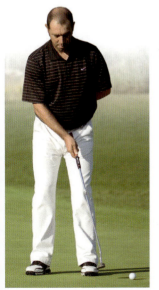

3 Think about pace rather than concentrating on a specific target. Have in mind an approximate distance, and try to group four or five balls as close together as possible.

❝ WHEN YOU REINTRODUCE YOUR LEFT HAND, YOUR STROKE WILL BE LESS INHIBITED. ❞

Stand against a wall to practise your stroke

If there are long intervals between each round you play, your game can become a little rusty. Often it is the short game, especially your putting, that is worst affected. This need not be the case, however. Between games, perform this simple indoor exercise based on the key subjects covered so far in this section: five minutes per day will be of enormous benefit to your game. You will soon notice a difference on the greens.

Head
Practising against a wall trains you to keep your head steady during the stroke

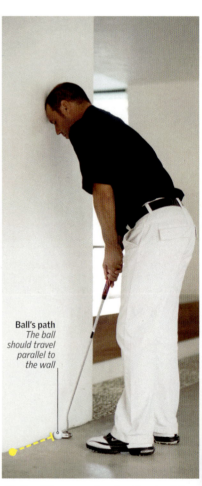

Ball's path
The ball should travel parallel to the wall

1 Take your putter and adopt your normal address position, with your head resting gently against any of the interior walls in your home. Drop a ball from the bridge of your nose. Wherever it lands is where you should position the ball (see Drill 3, p.134).

2 Now hit some medium-length – about 4m (4½yd) – putts along the wall. Keep an eye on the path of the putter relative to the straight line of the wall. The putterhead should initially travel straight back, gradually arcing inside as the backswing becomes longer. It should then return to square at impact, before tracking an inside path as the putter swings through.

Putt with a mirror for better results

Having your eyes directly over the ball at address is crucial for good putting action. From this position you can swivel your head for the perfect view down the intended line of the putt. This drill will not only ensure that your focus is directly over the ball but will also give you visual feedback on the alignment of the putter and its path.

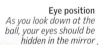

Eye position
As you look down at the ball, your eyes should be hidden in the mirror

1 Draw two lines on a small mirror: one vertical and one horizontal, so that they form a cross in the centre. Place the mirror on a flat surface. The horizontal line should point at the target.

2 Position a ball on the mirror, in the centre of the cross. At address, check your reflection. Your eyes should be hidden by the ball.

3 Line the putterface with the vertical line square to the target. With the other line, guide the putter on the correct path back and forth. Keep your head still in your swing.

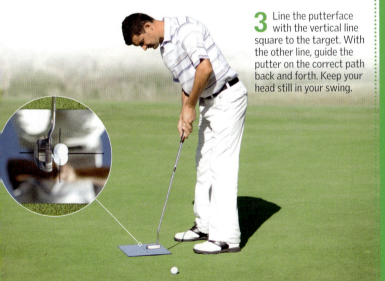

Try holing putts

If your putting is shaky from 1.5–2m (1½–2yd), start your practice routine by trying to hole putts of this length. This is because you will most likely miss more than you hole, which will lower your confidence. So before your next round, work on holing putts, not missing them.

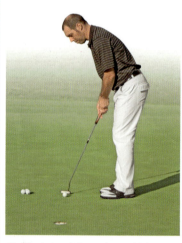

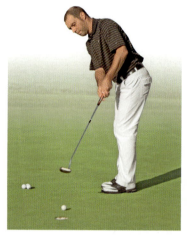

1 Start at a distance from which you feel confident. Although this distance is different for each golfer, you may want to start about 30cm (12in) from the hole.

2 Hit five or six balls into the back of the hole. Move back 15cm (6in). Using the same number of balls, repeat until you are about 1m (1yd) from the hole.

Hit to a smaller target

Visualization can have a wonderful effect on your game, as the following practice drill will illustrate. The exercise, which will give you a new perspective on holing-out, has maximum benefit if it is performed just before you start a round.

1 Place a coin on the green. Putt three or four balls towards the coin from a distance of 2m (2yd), so that each ball hits the coin.

COACHING TIP

With this drill, you can move further backwards and repeat the step. However, if you do try this exercise from a distance of more than 3m (3yd), you risk missing the coin so often that your confidence lowers, and you end up doing yourself more harm than good.

Every putt is a straight putt

Missing a breaking putt often results from not committing yourself to the line you chose. The slightest doubt usually manifests itself in a tentative stroke. The following exercise helps you avoid this tendency. It is based on the principle of treating every putt as a straight putt. Allowing the contours of the green to sweep the ball towards the hole simplifies the business of break putting.

1 Find a green with obvious slopes. Set yourself up with a putt about 5m (5¹/₂yd) from the hole. Read the green to see how much break there is on the putt. Decide on the line along which you want the ball to start. Visualize a secondary target on an extension of that line. So, on a putt where you see 30cm (12in) of right-to-left break, imagine a target 30cm (12in) to the right of the hole.

2 Make a few practice putting strokes, and focus on the imaginary target. Hit the putt at that target: the hole then becomes of secondary importance.

❝ IN THIS DRILL, **YOU ARE ALLOWING** THE CONTOURS OF THE GREEN **TO SWEEP THE BALL** TOWARDS THE HOLE. **❞**

Experiment with pace and line

Drill 15 (see p.143) suggested that judging breaking putts is not an exact science. There is always more than one line into the hole, and the route you choose depends on the amount of speed you apply to the ball (a softly struck putt breaks more than a putt struck firmly). The following exercise will reveal the relationship between pace and line, enhancing your visualization and touch on breaking putts.

1 Find a 4-m (4$\frac{1}{2}$yd) putt, where there is an obvious break from left-to-right or right-to-left.

2 Try to hole 3 or 4 putts from the same spot; hit each ball on a different line and vary the speed of the stroke. For example, with the first ball, try to "straighten" the putt by striking it firmly so that there is little break.

3 With the next putt, stroke the ball to trickle it into the hole, allowing for more break than with the previous shot. Try to hole putts while experimenting with different paces and lines.

Hit up-and-down putts to improve your speed

The main reason for three-putting is a poorly judged approach putt from long range. This is exacerbated when slopes come into play because golfers often struggle to adjust their stroke accordingly. The following exercise is designed to improve your judgement of speed, but it has the added difficulty of uphill and downhill putts.

1 Find a green with a pronounced slope across the putting surface. Place one tee-peg in the green 1m (1yd) short of the top of the slope and the other the same distance from the bottom of the slope, with a 12m (13yd) gap between the tee-pegs. Place three balls anywhere on the green and putt towards the tee-peg at the opposite end of the green.

SPEED IS EVERYTHING

To give your ball the optimum chance of dropping into the hole, the ball should move fast enough to travel 45–60cm (17$\frac{1}{2}$–24in) past the hole. This ensures that the ball holds its line as it approaches the hole, when subtle breaks can all too easily knock the putt off line.

RUNNING SPEED
The ideal pace for holing a putt is such that if the ball did miss, it would travel 45–60cm (17$\frac{1}{2}$–24in) beyond the hole.

2 Now putt the balls back towards the opposite tee-peg. Go backwards and forwards, putting the balls uphill and downhill.

Shotmaking

Sloping lies

The only place on a course where you can guarantee a totally level lie is on the teeing ground. Once off that manicured turf, you have to accept that the ball may well come to rest on a sloping lie, whether it be an upslope, a downslope, or a sideslope lie (where the ball is awkwardly positioned either above or below your feet).

Playing from a downslope
The slope deprives the club of its normal loft, and you may strike the turf before hitting the ball. So use a more lofted club, which decreases distance and gives a higher trajectory.

Left side
Put more of your weight to the left side

KEEP THE BALL BACK
Position the ball 5–10cm (2–4in) further back in your stance than it would be from a flat lie, to avoid heavy contact. Put slightly more weight on your front foot, and feel that your left shoulder is lower than for a regular shot.

45%

55%

Impact
There should be a descending blow into impact

CHASE THE BALL
Try not to lean back. Keep your weight distribution as it was at address. Then swing down the slope so that the clubhead chases after the ball through impact. Let your weight go with the clubhead's flow.

Ball position
The ball should be further back in your stance

LOFT ON SLOPES

When playing from an upslope, the clubface is effectively more lofted than if you were playing the same shot from a flat lie. A downslope effectively reduces the loft on the clubface, relative to the horizontal lie.

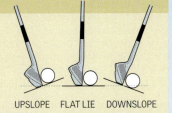

UPSLOPE   FLAT LIE   DOWNSLOPE

Playing from an upslope

This is the easier of the two up- and downslope lies. You can strike the ball cleanly, adding loft to the club, making the ball fly higher and shorter than from a flat lie. Again, you will need to "club-up". If the shot calls for a 6-iron from a flat lie, club-up to a 5-iron.

PREPARE FOR LAUNCH

Put the ball forward in your stance. Settle your weight on the lower foot, with an extra flex in your left leg. The ball tends to fly right-to-left from an upslope, so aim slightly right to compensate.

60%

40%

Impact
There should be a sweeping blow into impact

REMAIN STEADY

Keep your weight anchored over the right knee in your backswing. Your head should be steady as you swing down and you should feel that you swing the club up the slope.

Ball position
The slope decides how far forward should the ball be in your stance

Ball below your feet

This is the toughest of the sloping lies because it necessitates a swing from such an uncomfortable address position. The keys to success are establishing a balanced address position, and then maintaining your height through the hitting area. If you can do these two things, you should strike the ball solidly. However, you will not be able to make as powerful a swing as from a flat lie, therefore use a less-lofted club to make up the extra distance.

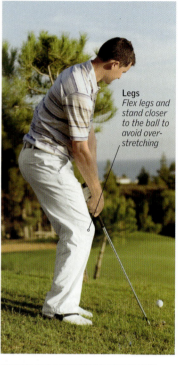

Legs
Flex legs and stand closer to the ball to avoid over-stretching

KEEP THE WEIGHT ON YOUR HEELS

When the ball is below your feet, adjust your posture to facilitate a solid strike. "Sit down" a little at address by flexing your knees, and widen your stance to further enhance your sense of balance. Because the ball is lower than usual, stand a fraction closer to it so that you are not overstretching. Because the ball will fly from left-to-right off this type of lie, aim left of the target to compensate.

SWING SMOOTHLY TO PROMOTE GOOD BALANCE

With sloping lies you must swing smoothly and not over-extend yourself. This is certainly the case when the ball is below your feet. Keep your knees flexed and make an "arms-dominated" swing to keep your balance. The slope tends to force your weight downhill, which can produce a shank (see p.165). To counter this problem, keep your weight back on your heels as you swing.

ADJUST THE CLUBFACE AIM

One of the effects of playing from above or below your feet is that the ball tends to deviate to the right or left through the air. You can allow for this by altering your alignment. But an alternative is to change the aim of the clubface. When the ball is above your feet, open the clubface to counter the ball's right-to-left flight. And when the ball is below your feet, close the clubface to fight the left-to-right flight path.

Ball above your feet

This is probably the easiest of all four sloping-lie shots, partly because the address position is comfortable but also because the slope does not hinder your ball-striking. What you need to be wary of is the ball-flight, which can be quite "hot" (less backspin and lots of forward momentum) from this type of lie. The ball also travels on a powerful right-to-left flight path. Therefore, it is wise to club-down to decrease distance and to aim right of the target.

STAND TALL; CHOKE DOWN

With this sort of shot, the ball is effectively raised. Therefore, on a severe slope, shorten the club by choking down on the grip and standing more erect at address. To maintain your balance as you swing, settle your weight a little more towards your toes.

> " ON A SEVERE SLOPE, **CHOKE DOWN** ON THE GRIP AND **STAND ERECT**. "

ALLOW FOR A ROUNDED SWING

From this kind of set-up and from this type of slope, your swing will be a little more rounded than usual. This means that your hands will not rise as high above your shoulders as with a regular swing. Other than that, there is nothing to worry about with this shot. Just make a smooth swing, maintaining your height and balance to produce a solid strike.

Grip
Choke down on the grip effectively to reduce the length of the club

Stance
Stand more upright than for a flat lie, with your weight more on your toes

Problem shots

The process of playing a successful shot from a problem spot is separated into three stages. Firstly, assess the lie of the ball and decide the effect it might have on your club selection. Secondly, if the target is within range, think where you want to pitch the ball, and envisage how the ball will react on landing. Thirdly, commit yourself to the shot you have elected to play, and trust the club you have chosen.

Shot from a bare lie

This is one of the toughest shots, and the closer you are to the green, the more difficult the task. The slightest mishit can be punished from a bare lie. So, the challenge here is to produce a clean strike, trapping the ball between the clubface and the ground.

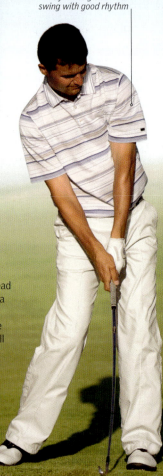

Rhythm
Maintain good balance by making a smooth swing with good rhythm

PRE-SET A CLEAN STRIKE
Never use a sand wedge from a bare lie, as the rounded sole bounces off the ground into the middle of the ball. To further promote a clean strike, position the ball roughly 2.5cm (1in) further back in your stance.

STEADY INTO IMPACT
As you make the shot, trust your set-up and swing to deliver the leading edge of the clubhead into the bottom of the ball. This should create a low trajectory but plenty of backspin because there is less interference between the clubface and ball at impact. This means that the ball will stop quickly on landing.

Playing out of a divot-mark

When your ball lands in an old divot-mark, the chances are it is when you have just hit a nice shot down the middle of the fairway. But unless the divot-mark is very deep, this is by no means a hopeless situation. Start by taking out a more-lofted club than if you were playing from the same distance with a good lie.

BALL BACK; HANDS FORWARD
Position the ball almost opposite your right heel and align your hands with your left thigh. This will promote an almost V-shaped swing, where the clubhead travels steeply into impact.

IT IS ALL IN THE WRISTS
To promote the necessary angle of attack in your downswing, hinge your wrists abruptly in your takeaway so that the club travels steeply upwards. Then hit down hard into the back of the ball.

Iron shot from thick rough

With light rough, allow for less backspin (as you cannot strike the ball cleanly). Thick rough limits your options. Determine the longest club you can hit, and try to reach the green with that; otherwise, play a well placed lay-up shot instead.

ORGANIZE YOUR SET-UP
Put the ball in the middle of your stance, and align your feet about 15–20 degrees left of the target.

PUNCH DOWN AND THROUGH
To further promote a steep attack, swing your hands up a little higher in your backswing. Then swing the clubhead steeply into the back of the ball.

Better wind play

A round of golf in the wind presents a greater challenge than playing on a calm day, but breezy conditions need not blow you off course. Assessing the conditions – knowing which way the wind is blowing – is something you will need to re-check as you work your way around the turns and contours of the course. But hitting the right shots for the conditions is ultimately what counts. Here are a handful of ideas that will improve your performance when the wind blows.

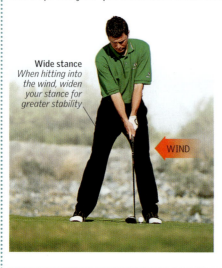

Wide stance
When hitting into the wind, widen your stance for greater stability

WIND

Swing smoothly off the tee

Move your feet 13cm (5in) further apart than normal for a solid strike. Do not tee the ball too low, as this often causes you to swing down more steeply. However, you should tee the ball a fraction lower than normal for a slightly lower flight (but focus on sweeping the ball away).

SOLID FOUNDATIONS
When playing in a strong wind, you may be blown off balance. Widening your stance gives you a more stable foundation.

Keep the ball low

There is no joy in playing a high ball into a strong wind. You will struggle to judge distance, the ball is easily blown off line, and you will have little control over the outcome of your shot. Therefore, keep the ball low and opt for a less-lofted club than you would otherwise use. If, for example, you are 135m (150yd) from the flag and that represents a normal 7-iron shot, club-up to a 5-iron.

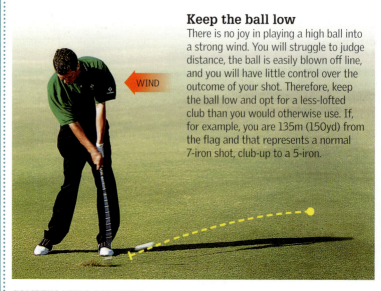

WIND

COMPENSATING FOR WIND
When playing a shot into the wind, club-up to produce a lower ball-flight, and remember the old adage: "swing with ease into the breeze".

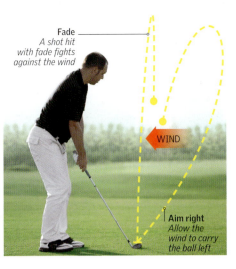

Fade
A shot hit with fade fights against the wind

WIND

Aim right
Allow the wind to carry the ball left

Shape your shot or adjust your aim

In a crosswind you have two options. If you are proficient at shaping the ball with sidespin, work the ball into the wind. Or else, play a straight shot in which you aim left or right of the target.

CROSSWINDS

In the right-to-left wind, you can either play a fade, so that the ball holds its line, or aim right and let the wind blow the ball towards the target.

Wind influences break and speed

Few golfers take into account the fact that a strong wind affects the ball's journey as it moves along the green. A crosswind either exaggerates or cancels out the break on a putt; a tail wind makes a putt run faster; and a headwind slows the ball down. You have to allow for these factors when you read each putt, even from short range. This becomes a bit of a balancing act, but, if you are aware of the wind's speed and direction, you can take steps to compensate for its effects.

WIND BREAK

A strong wind makes a difference to the break and speed of a putt, especially on fast, well-manicured putting surfaces. So do consider the wind's influence while putting.

Widen your putting stance

The act of putting involves such a precise movement that even the slightest buffeting from the wind can upset the path and pace of your stroke. Widen your stance by up to 50 per cent more than normal. Choke down on the grip so that you are more crouched over the ball. This lowers your centre of gravity. Hit a few putts.

REMAIN STEADY

If you widen your stance and choke down on the grip, you will find it easier to hold constant body and head positions.

How to hit high and low shots

There are occasions when it is desirable to manipulate the club's loft to work the ball into the flag on a higher or lower flight path. These shots will help you reach the proximity of the flag or achieve a well-placed lay-up shot when a conventional stroke could not.

Lofting the ball high

Launching the ball high into the air towards the target is a useful skill in certain situations. One such example is when you are playing downwind and want to maximize distance with a long iron. Another scenario might be when the flag is placed close to the front of the green and is guarded by a bunker: then you would want to bring the ball down from a greater height to encourage it to sit down quickly.

Head back
Your head should stay behind the ball for a little longer than usual through the hitting zone

Hands high
Finish the stroke with your hands held high

ADD LOFT TO THE CLUB
Use your normal club, and put the ball a little more forward in your stance; this increases the loft on the clubface by a few degrees. Stand erect and closer to the ball for a slightly more upright swing, which gives extra height on the ball-flight.

SWING NORMALLY AND FINISH HIGH
Now, you can make a regular swing. As you swing the club, ensure that your head stays behind the ball for longer than normal in the downswing and hitting zone. Also, in your followthrough, finish with your hands held high.

Punching the ball low

The "knockdown-punch shot", as it is often called, is suited to a variety of situations. As was mentioned in the section on wind play (see pp.154–55), this type of stroke is a great weapon to have at your disposal when playing into a strong headwind, helping the ball hold its line. It is also useful when you want to pitch a ball short of the green and let it run up to the flag.

REDUCE THE LOFT ON THE CLUB

The ball needs to go back in your stance by as much as three ball-widths, which delofts the clubface by several degrees. Also push your hands even further forward than normal so that the shaft is angled towards the target. In doing so, you have to be careful that the clubface does not become open. Turn in the toe of the clubhead slightly to ensure that the face is looking at the target. Your weight at address should be evenly spread.

Followthrough
Keep your followthrough low to reflect your desire to produce a low ball-flight

Torso
You should sense that your torso is over the ball as you sweep the ball away through the hitting zone

DRIVE THE BALL AND FINISH LOW

Try to sweep the club away low to the ground and make a shorter, more compact backswing than normal. Do not forget to turn your shoulders, though. Then, in your downswing, keep your torso over the ball at impact, and swing the clubhead low to the ground through the hitting zone. Again, your followthrough should reflect the ball-flight, so make sure your hands stay low in the finish.

Two simple ways to shape your shots

Ball-flight is determined by the clubhead's path in the swing and the aim of the clubface relative to this path. This imparts sidespin on the ball, which makes the ball deviate one way or the other. Controlling these impact factors allows you to shape your shots. the less loft here is on the club, the easier it is to shape the ball. This is because a relatively straight-faced club, which has little loft, imparts more sidespin than backspin on the ball making it easier to bend the flight of the ball. A lofted iron creates more backspin and less sidespin, reducing the bend on the ball. Also, you need a good lie to shape a ball.

Shaping shots with a draw

A draw is the perfect shot when the flag is located in the left corner of the green. Aiming straight at the target is risky because there is so little margin for error left of the flag. But, if you aim to the right of the flag and "draw" the ball in towards the target, the risks are less. If the ball flies straight, you hit middle of the green – no disaster there – and, if the ball draws according to plan, you are looking at a short putt.

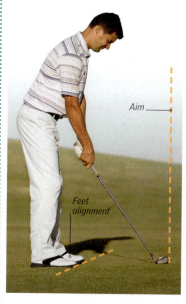

Aim

Feet alignment

ALIGN RIGHT; FACE SQUARE
If you want to swing the ball from right-to-left through the air, align your feet, hips, and shoulders right of the target. The more you want to draw the ball, the further right you stand. Then aim the clubface straight at the target. Also position the ball a little further back in your stance than is normal.

RELEASE THE CLUB AGGRESSIVELY
A draw requires an aggressive release of the club, whereby the right hand rolls over the left. The alignment of your stance encourages an in-to-out swing path through impact, parallel to the line of your feet. And, the clubface will be closed to this path at impact, imparting "draw-spin" on the ball.

Shaping shots with a fade

A fade is useful when dangers lurk on the right-hand side of the green (a bunker or water hazard, for example) or if the flag is tucked away on the right side. If the penalty for missing the green on the right side is more severe than missing it on the left, aiming to the left of the flag and playing a fade is the smart shot. If the stroke goes according to plan, you will finish close to the hole. If you stray slightly one side or other of the perfect line, you will most likely still hit the green. Even in the worst scenario, the ball will probably land to the left of the green, forcing you to make a straightforward chip onto the putting surface.

ALIGN LEFT; FACE SQUARE

To make the ball move on a left-to-right flight path, the address position is opposite to that required for a draw. Aim the clubface straight at the target, but align your feet, hips, and shoulders left of the target (essentially, an open stance). Also, position the ball a touch further forward in your stance at address – just one ball-width more than normal.

Aim

Feet alignment

USE AN OPEN CLUBFACE

The path of your swing through impact reflects your alignment, and so the clubhead swings along the line of your feet on an out-to-in path. The clubface will return to its position at address (open to this swing path), imparting sidespin so that the shot starts left and then fades right.

Faults and
Fixes

The slice

This is the most common fault of all – the bête noire of thousands of golfers the world over. A slice is a shot where the ball starts on a course to the left of the target and swerves, often quite dramatically, from left to right through the air. Because the problem is made more acute by a lack of loft, the biggest slices are hit with straight-faced clubs such as the driver, 3-wood, and long irons.

FAULT: POORLY ALIGNED SET-UP

It is hard to say which fault comes first – an open clubface or an out-to-in swing path. However, both these problems arise from a poor address position. The typical slicer is aligned to the left of the target, and the swing path simply follows the lines established at address. An open clubface at impact may be the result of not releasing the club properly (see pp.30–31). Soften your grip pressure for a free "swish".

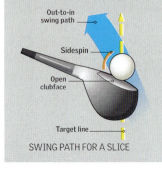

Out-to-in swing path

Sidespin

Open clubface

Target line

SWING PATH FOR A SLICE

FIX: TRAIN AN ON-LINE ATTACK

To cure a slice you must start by straightening your address position. Stand square to the target line, with your shoulders and feet in parallel alignment. This will promote a more correct path in your backswing. Then attempt to strike the ball so that it starts on a course to the right of the target line, encouraging an inside path of attack into impact. Also feel yourself rotating your forearms through impact to promote an aggressive release of the club. Together, these measures will help eradicate a slice.

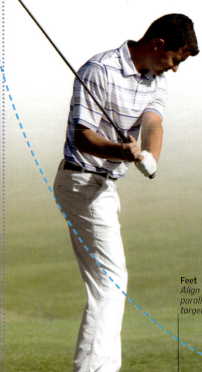

Feet
Align your feet parallel to the target line

Swing path
Maintain an inside line of attack in your downswing

The hook

This shot is described as the "good player's bad shot" because the hands are active through the hitting area. Yet, an incorrect swing path and closed clubface leave the ball flying well off line. The ball begins on a path to the right of the target and then moves right-to-left through the air. Due to a lack of loft, the biggest hooks occur with the driver.

FAULT: TRAPPED ON THE INSIDE

Typically with a hooked shot, the tendency is to slide your hips towards the target in your downswing. This leaves your hands, arms, and the club trapped too much on the inside. Instinctively, this feels as if the ball will fly to the right; to recover the situation, your hands become over-active, causing the shot to hook. Check your left-hand grip; you should be able to see only two knuckles. This should work the clubface into a neutral position at impact, culminating in a straighter ball-flight.

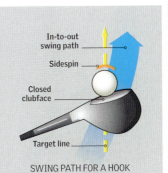

In-to-out swing path

Sidespin

Closed clubface

Target line

SWING PATH FOR A HOOK

FIX: CORRECT YOUR SWING PATH

To eliminate the excessive inside-the-line attack and to train an on-line swing path through impact, practise with an obstacle, such as a headcover, on the ground behind the ball and 15cm (6in) inside the target line. The obstruction blocks the path on which the clubhead swings into impact for a hook, forcing you to deliver the club to the ball on the correct path. While re-establishing a better swing path, concentrate on unwinding your hips, clearing them out of the way in your downswing, rather than sliding them towards the target.

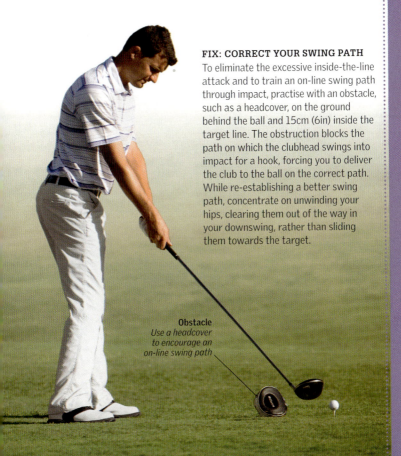

Obstacle
Use a headcover to encourage an on-line swing path

The "heavy-contact" chip

There is nothing in golf quite to match the ignominy of making a complete mess of a short shot, and the heavy-contact chip – a stroke in which heavy contact is made with the ground instead of the ball – ranks high in the embarrassment stakes. Somehow it is worse than missing a short putt and seemingly much harder to correct. However, the changes required to eliminate this shot are simple to apply.

FAULT: CLUB HITS THE GROUND BEFORE THE BALL
Heavy contact is the result of trying to help the ball into the air rather than letting the loft do the work. Employing a scooping action causes the clubhead to pass the hands prior to impact. In this shot, the clubhead buries itself in the ground, which absorbs most of the power in the shot. This means that hardly any energy is passed on to the ball.

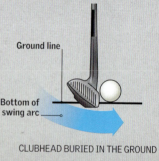

Ground line

Bottom of swing arc

CLUBHEAD BURIED IN THE GROUND

FIX: KEEP YOUR HANDS AHEAD OF THE CLUB
The desired ball-then-turf contact (see p.96) can only be achieved if you keep your hands in front of the clubhead into and through impact. To do this, as you start your downswing, maintain the angle in your right wrist – it should remain constant through the hitting zone. The bottom of the swing arc that has been formed should now coincide with the ball (see p.94), producing a clean strike and the smallest of divots after impact.

The shanked iron shot

The shank is probably the most destructive shot you can hit on the course. The ball shoots off the club at an angle of at least 45 degrees to the target, often never to be seen again. You can hit a shank with any iron, but, whatever the club, once the damage is done, it cannot be easily remedied.

FAULT: POOR LINE OF ATTACK

With a shanked shot, the ball is hit from the hosel. For that to happen, the clubhead must be further away from your body at impact than at address. This is caused by "throwing" the clubhead away from your body at the start of your downswing, so that it swings through the hitting zone on an out-to-in path. Because of the shape of the hosel, the ball flies almost sideways to the line of play – a highly destructive fault.

Out-to-in swing path

Hosel

Target line

SWING PATH FOR A SHANK

FIX: BLOCK THE PATH TO A SHANK

To eliminate the destructive path of attack into impact, place an obstacle behind the ball, 8cm (3in) outside the target line. Then hit a shot with a short iron. The obstacle makes it necessary for you to swing the club towards the ball on the correct path, leading to solid contact between the sweet spot and the ball.

Obstacle
Place a ball-box just outside the ball-to-target line to prevent an out-to-in swing path

Clubface
With the club on the correct path, there is solid contact between the sweet spot and the ball

The skied drive

The skied drive is not the most damaging of shots – indeed, the ball tends to fly reasonably straight, which means you rarely lose a ball. You do, however, lose as much as 70 per cent of the normal distance for any given club. A skied drive occurs when the clubhead chops down steeply under a ball that is teed up (occasionally too high).

FAULT: STEEP DOWNSWING ATTACK

A skied drive is the result of picking the club up too steeply with your hands in your takeaway. This promotes a narrow swing arc, and the downswing becomes a product of your poor backswing. When the top-edge of the clubhead makes contact with the bottom portion of the ball, the ball shoots up into the air but with little forward momentum.

The shot is the result of a very steep angle of attack into impact. It is most common with the driver and 3-wood.

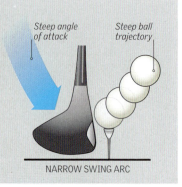

Steep angle of attack

Steep ball trajectory

NARROW SWING ARC

FIX: START YOUR TAKEAWAY LOW AND SLOW

To promote a shallower angle of attack, widen your backswing arc. Concentrate on sweeping the club away "low and slow", turning your back on the target (see p.42), and swinging your arms and the club around your body more. This promotes a backswing that is full and wide. In the downswing, focus on sweeping the ball away rather than hitting down on it.

Body motion
Turn your shoulders and arms around your body for a rounded swing

Wide backswing
A wide backswing arc in your takeaway promotes a shallow angle of attack in your downswing

Saucer-shaped arc
Think of the club travelling back on a saucer-shaped arc

The top

The top is generally looked upon as a beginner's fault, but it also afflicts experienced players. Whatever your standard, it is an embarrassing shot because the outcome looks pathetic. The clubhead clips the top of the ball, sending it scuttling along the ground. It occurs most with either a drive or a fairway-wood shot.

FAULT: GAINING HEIGHT IN SWING
If you top a shot, you are raising your posture in your swing, which brings up the bottom of your swing arc to the point where the clubhead is close to missing the ball.

Bottom of swing arc

CLUBHEAD STRIKING THE BALL'S TOP

Impact
If you maintain your original height in the swing, you are more likely to generate solid contact

Posture
Maintain your spine angle from address until impact

FIX: MONITOR YOUR POSTURE FROM ADDRESS TO IMPACT
Whichever fault is causing you to top the ball, the conclusion is the same. You have to make sure that you maintain good posture from address until the point of impact. Adopt a good posture (see pp.28–29) and address a tee-peg with your driver. Now make practice swings, trying to clip the tee-peg out of the ground while maintaining your spine angle throughout your backswing and through the hitting zone. Then tee up a ball and hit some drives, working on the same principles. Concentrate on solid contact rather than distance.

The push shot

The end result of a push shot is the same as a slice: the ball finishes way off to the right. But the cause is different. Whereas the slice begins on a leftward path and swerves to the right through the air, the push starts on a path to the right and stays right. This can happen with any club, and it is not necessarily caused by a poorly struck shot.

FAULT: HITTING FROM IN-TO-OUT

A push is the result of the clubhead swinging into the ball on an exaggerated in-to-out path, with the clubface square to that path. These factors cause the ball to fly in a direct line, albeit one that is off the course. If the clubface is open to this path, the ball swerves further to the right.

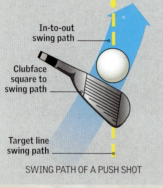

In-to-out swing path

Clubface square to swing path

Target line swing path

SWING PATH OF A PUSH SHOT

FIX: TRAIN AN ON LINE ATTACK

The key to curing a push is to eliminate the excessive inside path of attack. Address the ball with your left toe in line with your right heel. Because your left side is already cleared out of the way (due to the very open stance), you have room to swing the club more to the left through impact. Once you have played a shot this way, try to recreate that swing from a normal stance. You should find that the ball sets off straight at the target, the sign of an on line swing path.

Swing path
With your left side out of the way, it is easier to correct an in-to-out swing path

Open stance

Normal feet alignment

The pull shot

A pull is the opposite of a push. The ball starts on a leftward path, because of an out-to-in swing path. It then continues on that path because the clubface is square to the out-to-in line of attack. As with the push, it can happen with any club, from a driver down to a wedge.

FAULT: CLUBHEAD OUTSIDE THE LINE

In this shot, your hands and arms move too far away from your body at the start of your downswing. As with a slice, a pull shot is the product of an out-to-in swing path. But, whereas a slice occurs if the clubface is open, a pull occurs if the clubface is square to the out-to-in path. (Note: if the clubface is closed to this path, the result is what is known as a pull-hook. This shot starts left of the target and curves even further to the left in the air – a wild shot indeed.)

Out-to-in swing path

Clubface square to swing path

Target line swing path

SWING PATH OF A PULL SHOT

FIX: DEVELOP AN INSIDE ATTACK

In curing a pull, try to appreciate the sensation of the clubhead approaching the ball from inside the target line. Draw your right foot back from this line so that your right toe is level with your left heel (your shoulders must stay square). This promotes a fuller body turn, and creates space for the club to travel on an inside path during your downswing.

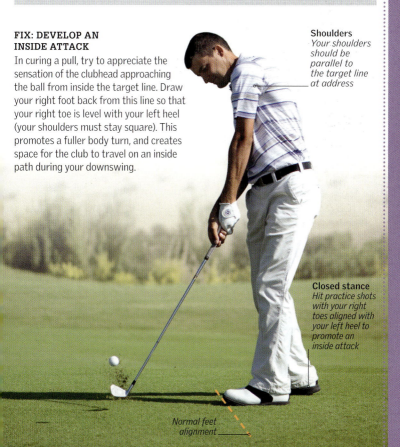

Shoulders
Your shoulders should be parallel to the target line at address

Closed stance
Hit practice shots with your right toes aligned with your left heel to promote an inside attack

Normal feet alignment

Glossary

Address Another word used to describe a golfer's *set-up*.

Albatross A score of three under *par* on one *hole*.

Approach shot A stroke played with the intention of hitting the *green*.

Apron of the green The closely mown area of grass between the *rough* and the putting surface.

Bare lie A situation in which the ball is sitting on a patch of ground with very little or no grass on it at all.

Birdie A score of one under *par* on one *hole*.

Blade A forged iron clubhead that offers superior feel at impact, but is less forgiving to off-centre strikes. Also the bottom edge of an iron.

Bogey A score of one over *par* on one *hole*. Also a *matchplay* competition played against the par of the course.

Bounce The wide flange at the base of a sand wedge.

Break The deviation left or right made by a ball rolling along a *green* due to slopes on the putting surface.

Carry The distance a ball flies through the air.

Cavity back An iron with the back of the head hollowed out, which positions weight around the perimeter of the clubhead. This increases the mass behind off-centre strikes.

Closed stance An *address* position in which the golfer's alignment is to the right of the target.

Clubbing down A situation in which a golfer takes a more-lofted club, for example an 8-iron instead of a 7-iron.

Clubbing up A situation in which a golfer takes a less-lofted club, for example a 5-iron instead of a 6-iron.

Collar of rough The area of grass where the *apron of the green* joins the *rough*.

Divot The turf dislodged at impact while playing a shot.

Divot-mark The hole in the ground left as a result of a *divot* being taken.

Driver The longest club in the bag, designed for hitting tee shots.

Eagle A score of two under *par* on one *hole*.

Fade When the ball moves from left to right through the air, due to sidespin imparted at impact.

Fairway The closely mown area of grass bordered on either side by longer grass *(rough)*.

Fourball betterball A competition played in pairs, in which the best score of the two partners on each *hole* counts.

Foursomes A game of pairs in which two golfers share the same ball, one teeing off on odd-numbered holes, the other on even-numbered holes. After the tee shot the pair play alternate shots.

Green The putting surface. (The *hole* is located on the green.)

Greensomes A type of play in which partners both tee off on each *hole*. They then select the more favourable of the two balls and play alternate shots with the same ball until the hole is completed.

Grip The rubber handle at the top of a club. Also, both hands positioned on the grip.

Grounding the club Resting the clubhead on the ground behind the ball at *address*.

Halved In a *matchplay* competition, if *opponents* register the same score on a *hole*, the hole is said to be "halved".

Handicap A figure that reflects a golfer's ability relative to the par of the course.

Heavy A shot in which the clubhead strikes the ground before the ball.

Heel The area of the clubface nearest to the *shaft* of the club.

Hole The hole itself (which is located on the *green*). Also a general term for describing the area between the *teeing ground* and the green, for example: "the first hole".

Hook A shot in which the ball moves right-to-left due to sidespin imparted at impact. An exaggerated version of a draw.

Hosel The part of the clubhead into which the *shaft* is secured.

Lie Where the ball comes to rest on the course. Also, the angle at which the bottom edge of the clubhead sits relative to the *shaft*.

Loft The angle at which the clubface sits relative to perpendicular. This determines the ball's *trajectory*.

Loose impediment A term used in the Rules of Golf to describe a movable natural object, such as a leaf or twig, interfering with the line of play.

Matchplay A game played between single *opponents* or pairs in which *holes* are won, lost, or *halved*.

Obstruction A term from the Rules of Golf to describe an artificial object that might interfere with play, such as a fixed sprinkler head (an immovable obstruction) or empty can (a moveable obstruction).

Open stance An *address* position in which the golfer's alignment is to the left of the target.

Opponent A person whom you play against in a *matchplay* situation.

Out-of-bounds A designated area of a golf course where play is permanently not permitted. The penalty for hitting a ball out-of-bounds is *stroke and distance*.

Par The standard score for a *hole*, based on the number of shots an accomplished player would normally take to complete the hole. Also a score equal to the par on a hole.

Par 3 A *hole* that should be completed in three strokes. To achieve *par*, usually the *green* should be hit in one stroke, followed by two putts.

Par 5 A long *hole*, which should be completed in five strokes. To achieve *par*, usually the *green* should be hit in three strokes.

Pivot The coiling and uncoiling of the upper body in the swing, combined with the correct *weight transfer*.

Posture The overall position of the body and legs in the *set-up*.

Preferred lies A local rule often introduced during the winter months when ground conditions are usually poor. The rule permits golfers to move their ball on to a more favourable *lie*, so long as this is within 15cm (6in) of the spot where the ball originally came to rest. The rule usually only applies on closely mown areas of grass, such as the *fairway* or the *apron of the green*.

Pull A shot in which the ball starts left of target and continues to fly in that direction.

Push A shot in which the ball starts right of target and continues to fly in that particular direction.

Reading a putt The process of studying the line of a putt to identify possible breaks that might occur as the ball moves towards the *hole*.

Releasing the club A phrase describing how the right hand rolls over the left through impact, indicating a powerful and free swing of the clubhead.

Rough The thicker grass either side of the *fairway* and around most *greens*. The rough is designed to penalize wayward shots: it

is more difficult to play from than the closely mown grass of the fairway.

Run The portion of a ball's journey from the time the ball first hits the ground to the point where it eventually comes to rest. More lofted clubs produce less run; less-lofted clubs, such as the *driver* and long irons, tend to generate more run.

Scratch A *handicap* of zero.

Set-up The position you adopt before striking the ball, including your *grip, aim, stance*, and *posture*. Also known as the *address*.

Shaft The part of a club between the *grip* and the clubhead.

Shank A shot in which the ball is struck from the *hosel* of the club, causing the ball to fly sharply to the right of the target.

Sky A tee shot played with either a *driver* or lofted wood in which the top edge of the clubhead strikes the bottom of the ball, which flies steeply upwards.

Slice A shot in which the ball moves from left-to-right through the air as a result of sidespin imparted at impact. An exaggerated version of a *fade*.

Splash shot A bunker shot in which the clubhead strikes the sand behind the ball, and a wave of sand propels the ball out of the bunker.

Stableford A type of play in which points are awarded according to the score relative to *par* on each *hole*. The golfer with the maximum points after 18 holes is the winner.

Stance The width your feet are apart at *address*, and the position of the ball relative to your feet.

Stroke and distance A penalty in which the golfer must return to the spot from which the last

stroke was played (conceding the distance gained) and add one stroke to their score for that *hole*.

Strokeplay A type of play in which each competitor records his or her score for each *hole*. The golfer with the lowest total is the winner.

Sweet spot The centremost portion of the clubface, where the majority of the clubhead's mass is located.

Tee A common abbreviation, referring to either a *tee-peg* or the *teeing ground* itself.

Teeing area The part of the *teeing ground* from which golfers must hit tee shots. The teeing area is two club-lengths deep and its width is defined by two tee markers.

Teeing ground The whole area of closely mown grass on which the designated *teeing area* is situated.

Tee-peg The implement on which a ball sits during the process of hitting a tee shot.

Toe The area of the clubface furthest from the *shaft* of the club.

Tour event A professional tournament usually played over four rounds, in which the golfer with the lowest 72-hole score is the winner.

Trajectory The arc on which the ball flies through the air. Higher-numbered irons, which have more *loft*, propel the ball on a higher trajectory. Lower-numbered irons, which have less loft, send the ball on a lower trajectory.

Utility wood A lofted metal-wood, such as a 7-wood, that features a small clubhead. Utility woods are designed for advancement shots from the *fairway* and light *rough*.

Weight transfer The process whereby the weight of the body moves from one foot to the other during the process of swinging a club.

Index

Acknowledgments

Dorling Kindersley would like to thank the following people for their help in the preparation of this book: Gerard Brown and Nigel Wright for the photographs; Adam Brackenbury for creative technical support; and Margaret McCormack for indexing.

Picture credits

The publisher would like to thank the following for their permission to reproduce their photographs:

(Key: b-below/bottom; c-centre; l-left; r-right; t-top; cl-centre left; cr-centre right)

6–7 Getty Images (br); 13 Getty Images (b);
34–35 Visions in Golf (cl) (c) (cr) (t) (cr);
50–51 Visions in Golf (cl) (c) (cr) (t) (cr);
68–69 Getty Images (tr) (bl) (tr) (b);

72–73 Visions in Golf (cl) (c) (cr) (t) (cr);
90–91 Visions in Golf (cl) (c) (cr) (t) (cr);
108–09 Visions in Golf (cl) (c) (cr) (t) (cr);
130–31 Visions in Golf (cl) (c) (cr) (t) (cr);
154–55 Getty Images (tl) (b) (bl)

All other images © Dorling Kindersley

For further information see:
www.dkimages.com